Secrets of successful
CEOs

Insights into life, leadership and business

Compliments of

TEC® CHIEF EXECUTIVES WORKING TOGETHER | better leaders **decisions** results

THE WORLD'S LEADING CHIEF EXECUTIVE ORGANIZATION

WWW.TEC-CANADA.COM

First Published 2007

© Copyright 2007 Adrian Geering

Published by 100x Publishing

PO Box 320, Unley, SA 5061, Australia

www.secretsofceos.com

National Library of Australia Cataloguing-in-Publication Data:

Geering, Adrian D. (Adrian Douglas).

Secrets of successful CEOs.

1st ed. ISBN 978-0-9803397-0-3

Geering, Adrian D.
1. Chief executive officers.
2. Chief executive officers - Interviews.
3. Executive ability.
4. Leadership.
I.Title.

658.4092

Project managed by Messenger Publishing

Photography: Jay Geering

Secrets of successful

CEOs

Insights into life, leadership and business

Adrian Geering PhD, MCC, CHIC

www.secretsofceos.com

CONTENTS

CEOs

Acknowledgements

This book was conceived during a significant moment in Sydney in June, 2006 when Matt Church of Thought Leaders challenged me to begin to document my extensive experience with CEOs. The research and writing of this edition took place between August 2006 and April 2007.

I am indebted to the support and encouragement of a range of people and would like to acknowledge their contribution: Louise Hertling and Sheri Cleveley for their excellent assistance in typing the manuscript; Lisa Messenger and Mel Carswell for their assistance in coordinating the project and their wonderful input and encouragement; my son, Jay Geering, for his excellent photography and input on the book; and my wife, Marie Geering, for her fastidious proof reading, challenging the design and structure of the book and encouraging me to complete the task.

Above all, I wish to thank the 20 contributors for their willing involvement, feedback and support for the project.

Dedication

Dr Phil Meddings, founder of The Executive Connection (TEC) in Australia, my mentor colleague and friend.

I first met Phil Meddings in 1985 when he invited me to start a CEO mentoring group in Adelaide (in conjunction with TEC) which came to pass in 1987.

I dedicate this book to Phil because his great vision, wisdom, integrity, support, encouragement and friendship enabled me to make the wonderful journey of mentoring and coaching CEOs.

For this, I will be forever grateful.

Foreword

The Australian corporate sector over the years has provided a superb array of effective and dynamic leaders. In this book, Adrian Geering has successfully identified those who stand tall. He has researched the arena well and analysed the best of the best. The quality and calibre of leaders included in this book validate that he has had a close and personal relationship with each one of them.

I commend the breadth of leadership showcased in this book. It conveys the message that true leadership makes a valuable contribution to society and that effective living is a dialogue between an individual and his strengths, and the world that needs them. It is encouraging to see so many who have built on their islands of strength and have had the courage to use them to shape and empower others.

A leader sets the pace, defines the landscape, identifies the voids, marks the path that others may follow, makes the tough calls and decisions and is ready to be held accountable. A leader also sees the future before it arrives: he takes on the significant challenge to deal with situations which are inevitable but not imminent and recognises that what looms ahead may be of more serious consequence than that which has already arrived. A leader is more than a thermometer of society's trends and needs; he is more like a thermostat – measuring the temperature and responding accordingly.

Leadership is a journey from isolation to connection where good leaders build on people's strength and help them make their weaknesses irrelevant. Leaders make space for others to excel. It requires a desire to have an impact and introduce positive change. A leader derives his greatest joy and sense of personal achievement in seeing something that enables and empowers others. A leader does not strive for ownership for its sake alone but looks at the transformation his style will have on society at large.

It is my hope that in this book, readers will find the encouragement and inspiration to, in turn, inspire and empower many others within their sphere of influence. I hope it will encourage readers to make a positive difference, as I know Adrian and those described in this book certainly have.

I compliment the author for his initiative in publishing this book. It is a new and refreshing perspective on a topic that powerfully impacts on each one of us.

David Bussau, founder of Opportunity International Australia, co-founder of the Opportunity International Network and winner of the 2003 Ernst & Young Australian Entrepreneur of the Year Award

September 2007

Introduction: Why This Book?

This book was written from the perspective of my life: 20 years experience living and working in my parents' businesses during my youth, 20 years writing and thinking about business, and a further 20 years running several of my own businesses. My experiences working with Chief Executive Officers (CEOs) in the capacity of mentor, coach, adviser, strategic consultant and trainer have provided me with unique insight into the behaviours and attitudes of these highly successful individuals. By sharing their stories and personal views on how to develop and magnify success, I hope to encourage and inspire you in your own endeavours.

Secrets of Successful CEOs arose from my previous two books: *A Guide to Principles and Practices of Human Resource Management* and *Business Diagnostics*. After working on these it became clear that it was important to write about the secrets of successful CEOs using my insider knowledge and contacts.

I have personally worked with about 75 CEOs over the past 20 years in both personal and group mentoring. Some of my clients have been with me for almost two decades and it has been a privilege to watch them develop outstanding businesses, leveraging their success 100X. The metrics of this work are interesting – about 18,000 hours of mentoring and coaching one-on-one, and 600 days conducting group mentoring programs with 16 or more CEOs per group.

My experience of working with CEOs covers a range of activities including: acting as Chairman of two CEO groups with The Executive Connection (TEC) since 1987; working as a Senior Certified E-Myth Consultant and presenting Michael Gerber's E-Myth Mastery program to 20 clients over nine years; working as a Chartered Management Consultant over the past 20 years in a wide range of companies and industries – facilitating 110 strategic plans (5 – 10 days each); completing 63 enterprise reviews (5 – 10 days each), 25 diagnostic studies, restructuring numerous companies and carrying out a range of other activities including mentoring CEOs and Boards, Chairing and acting as a Director for several companies; speaking to CEOs around Australia, the UK, Malaysia and USA; and training and mentoring TEC Chairs for the past 12 years in Australia, Malaysia, Europe and USA.

By writing this book I hope to document the successes of Australian CEOs – there are very few Australian examples and case studies to be found in business books, especially from SMEs (small-to-medium enterprises). I have focused my life on working and studying in this area and thus have an important contribution to make.

My primary aim in life is to be a leader motivated by love and dedicated to making a difference in the lives of many people. Many of my life goals relate to this ideal: to leave a legacy that is timeless and universally useful; to be an intuitive, energetic mental pioneer and creator in developing new ideas; to continue my love affair with words, writing and speaking to explore and reveal some of the secrets of life; to continue using my skills in mentoring leaders; and to teach leadership and personally develop and influence others. My hope is that this book will go some way towards fulfilling these goals.

I also have a passionate commitment to action learning and have been focused on this for 30 years. True learning relates to taking action, reflecting on action and then taking more action. The majority of CEOs (and most other people) do not do what they know. I am committed to assisting people to leverage their lives, leadership and businesses 100X – the focus of my new business. Leverage relates to the concept of multiplying your resources through working with others in a win-win situation. It is a means of using the concept of compound interest to accomplish your purpose with great power and influence.

Lastly, this is not a clever compilation book written to be a glossy addition to your desk or coffee table. This book has been written out of the crucible of intentional mentoring and coaching. It is thus quite different from any other book pertaining to this topic, as the author has lived the experiences of each of the CEOs involved and shared their celebrations, joy and pain. It is an honest and open account of the secret strategies that successful CEOs employ.

What are Secrets?

A secret is something that very few people know about – it is hidden knowledge. Why write about secrets of CEOs? Because you are not likely to learn this important information any other way. CEOs usually never share their secrets because: they work in a very competitive environment and, naturally, keep things close to their chests; they are usually not in a regular confidential peer group meeting to share these things; they don't generally speak to others about such matters and may feel threatened in doing so; they sometimes don't view the information as secret material and therefore don't see the importance of sharing it; they don't want to lose face publicly and prefer to keep their problems hidden.

What is Success?

From my mentoring experience, I have discovered that one of the most interesting areas to focus on with CEOs is their problems, which are usually perceived to be caused externally. Rarely do they see initially that many of their problems are caused by themselves: lack of focus; lack of discipline; lack of accountability including poor time management and unclear priorities; poor decisions; lack of balance; poor relationships; lack of personal and professional growth; lack of goals; isolation; lack of implementation; lack of support; lack of a sounding board; lack of sharing; lack of honest feedback; and lack of results. Another major factor is that they may not want to make themselves vulnerable in order to grow and become successful, which leads us to the question, "What is success?"

Success is defined as favourable results, a wished-for ending, good fortune, accomplishing what is desired or intended, and gaining wealth, position or other advantage. Whatever success is and however you define it, one thing is certain: it is quite often elusive. It is about your values and letting your life speak through demonstration of results. To some people, it is simply making a lot of money but this is clearly a very limited view of success.

Perhaps it is more easily described by discussing what it is not. It is not wealth alone, as this is so limited and one-dimensional. Having money to give you choice is important, however, it is how you use your wealth that makes the difference. There are many wealthy people who are not rich in a broad and philosophical sense; they focus on greed and may be characterised

by selfishness, dishonesty, sadness, emptiness and pettiness. They may have money, but their persistent self-focus and conceited opinions do not reflect genuine, all-encompassing success. Their lives focus on lack, lawsuits, fraud, legalism and strife – a true win-lose approach. Such people can certainly not be viewed as holistically successful.

True success and true wealth is about using money for altruism – this is typified by noble character, fulfillment, joy, happiness, honesty and selflessness. People who have this focus are truly wealthy and successful because they focus on innovation, benevolence, tithing, expansion, new opportunities, value for money, true service and generosity – a true win-win position.

These two approaches reflect different value orientations and underpin the lives of all people, including CEOs. So, when we examine "Secrets of Successful CEOs" in each chapter, we need to view them from this context.

Another major factor in being a successful CEO relates to leadership and personal style. It is not a bullying, autocratic style or winning by intimidation that leads to permanent success. A senior manager said to me recently, "I know some CEOs who are pigs in the way they treat their staff". He was describing his own CEO, having stayed and put up with aggressive bullying, harassment and abuse because of what he was paid. How sad! Such tyrants will only prosper in the short term, because abusive behaviour is destructive and detrimental to all involved.

It is not about manipulating the political system, as happens in so many bureaucracies – many CEOs are appointed by a representative committee structured to give the right political outcome. It is also not about being laissez-faire and letting powerful others dominate and take over the agenda. It is about being a captain or coach, a servant, a Level 5 leader (*Good to Great,* by Jim Collins); someone who is always building the team and helping others to become leaders themselves.

How do successful CEOs operate as leaders? With vision, passion, dedication and great action. They understand internally what is happening by reviewing the business and setting a clear action plan and direction strategy. They lead as mentors, conducting excellent meetings, powerful one-on-ones and keeping their team accountable through a well structured strategic plan, annual business plan, 90-day plans and clear key performance indicators. They are clear, simple and direct, focusing on a few key goals. They are passionate about the strategy of the company and about building a winning team with top people in every key position. They are always focusing on the external environment and know where their industry is, who their competitors are, and how their brand is developing. They provide superior customer service and are keen to innovate, create and continuously improve what they are doing. They are always speaking to their suppliers and bankers and influencing all of the major stakeholders in their business.

Above all, they are keen to run best-practice winning companies with excellent results for customers, staff, external stakeholders and shareholders. What are the characteristics of best-practice winning companies? Many things, but this will be the focus of another book. In the meantime, remember what Calvin Coolidge said about success: "Nothing in this world can take the place of persistence. Talent will not; nothing is more common than unsuccessful men with talent. Genius will not; unrewarded genius is almost a proverb. Education will not; the world is full of educated derelicts. Persistence and determination alone are omnipotent."

How to Read This Book:

This book contains 19 case studies profiling 20 excellent Chief Executive Officers (CEOs) from a wide range of industries, each in different stages of an organisation's life cycle.

The order in which you read this material depends on where you are now in your career and business, and therefore what needs you currently have. For your convenience, I have grouped the chapters into four themes so you can easily identify which chapters will be most relevant and helpful to your particular circumstances. These themes are: starting and growing a business; developing and maturing a business; operating a family business; and operating a national and /or global business.

1. Starting and Growing a Business

Five CEOs are profiled in this section:

John Chataway from **Kojo** – a study of how to start and grow a company composed of eight interlinked diverse businesses focusing on anything related to the electronic screen, with an annual turnover of $12 million.

Andrew Downs from **SAGE Automation** – a story focused on establishing and growing a business in the automation area from a one-person operation to $40 million in ten years.

Frances Guyett from **RDDT** – a story about the transformation of a small university-based business developing from a start-up into a private company.

Scott Hicks from **Adam Internet** – a picture of a Generation Y CEO establishing a significant company in the Internet business – a company that originally started out as a schoolboy hobby is now a $21 million business.

Terri Scheer from **Terri Scheer Insurance Brokers** – this chapter details the courage of a single mother starting and growing a business with guts and determination, and developing it into a significant, highly recognised company that enjoys a $23 million turnover.

2. Developing and Maturing a Business

Five CEOs from mature companies make up this stable:

First is **Greg Connor** from **Savings and Loans Credit Union** – we look at why it has become recognised as Australia's leading credit union and how it has grown from $650 million assets to $2 billion assets under Greg's leadership.

Bob Day's company **Home Australia** – a study of how a successful entrepreneur uses his wealth and success to help others. Having grown his company from a $50 million state-based operation to a large national group of companies achieving sales of $200 million, Bob is now able to philanthropically support his staff and community.

Nigel McBride of **Minter Ellison** – this chapter provides an interesting punctuation in the book. Nigel came to Adelaide and did what no one else has ever done – doubled a law practice in four years to secure an annual turnover of $36 million.

Mike Rungie for **ACH Group** – here we have a picture

of a well-run not-for-profit aged care business, which has grown to $54 million yet still retains its focus of serving older people.

Ian Stirling of **ElectraNet** – a study of a monopolistic private infrastructure company formed from part of a former government enterprise. The company, with sales of $200 million (90% of which is provided by government regulation) is a good study of how to transform a culture from that of a government organisation to that of a commercial enterprise.

3. Operating a Family Business

Five family businesses are presented in this group:

John Angove of **Angove's** – an interesting case study of success in a five-generation family winery, detailing how the company has grown to $49 million in a highly competitive industry.

Roger Drake of **Drake Food Markets** – this is the story of how a simple grocer developed a $560 million business from a single store and founded a family dynasty.

Joe Grilli of **Primo Estate Wines** – a presentation of how a family developed a creative and artistic business based on fine wines and the good life. The company started from the humble beginnings of a $1 million turnover, growing to a strong niche business of $4 million.

In stark contrast is the chapter on **Richard Hamood** of **Lenard's** – this compelling case study discusses the development of a successful family business based around franchising, and the challenge Richard experienced facing a legal battle which almost destroyed the $20 million company.

Anthony Toop and **Karen Raffen** of **Toop & Toop Real Estate** – this chapter covers the difficult transition in a family-owned business of handing over leadership to an outsider. We hear from both parties about how the change was smoothly managed to ensure this high-performing real estate agency continued its previous success – the company now has an annual turnover of $10 million.

4. Operating a National and/or Global Business

This section provides overviews of four CEOs who manage groups of companies that operate in a national and/or global market.

Doug Brown of **Entech** – Entech is a company that has found the secret of surviving in a declining industry in Australia; through going global the company has grown to a $45 million operation.

Kim Scott of **Electronic Systems Group** (part of Tenix Defense) – an overview of a niche business with global potential in diverse, related niche markets, with a revenue base of $52 million.

Chris Stathy of **Philmac** – this chapter demonstrates how an Australian manufacturer, as part of a global group, can move from an $70 million base to become a significant global player.

Glen Simpson of **Coffey International Development** – an inside look at a successful public company acquisition, which has grown CID from a $30 million local company to a $100 million global business.

General Hints

You may like to use some or all of the 20 CDs which were packaged with this book (and the associated study guide) as a monthly staff/management development tool. Whatever you choose to do will depend on you but the benefits that will accrue when you apply the most important points from a case study to your personal situation should result in continuous change, ongoing improvement and significant development in your company. Are you ready for success?

Here are a number of "reading routes" you may like to follow:

Route 1   If you are Starting and Growing a Business

First read Theme 1 – Starting and Growing a Business

Next read Theme 3 – Operating a Family Business

Then read Theme 2 – Developing and Maturing a Business

Lastly read Theme 4 – Operating a National and/or Global Business

Route 2   **If you are Operating a Family Business**

First read Theme 3 – Operating a Family Business

Next read Theme 1 – Starting and Growing a Business

Then read Theme 2 – Developing and Maturing a Business

Lastly read Theme 4 – Operating a National and/or Global Business

Route 3   **If you are Operating a Mature Business**

First read Theme 2 – Developing and Maturing a Business

Next read Theme 4 – Operating a National and/or Global Business

Then read Theme 3 – Operating a Family Business

Lastly read Theme 1 – Starting and Growing a Business

Route 4   **If you are Operating a Global Business**

Firstly read Theme 4 – Operating a National and/or Global Business

Next read Theme 2 – Developing and Maturing a Business

Then read Theme 1 – Starting and Growing a Business

Lastly read Theme 3 – Operating a Family Business

When the factors to success mentioned earlier are applied deliberately or intentionally they leverage a company incredibly, as has happened with the examples discussed in this book.

However, the key to having 100X leverage comes from high impact mentoring, advising and teaching to help CEOs gain clarity of purpose, maintain accountability and facilitate the implementation of processes to meet that purpose. The compound effect of focusing on the three areas of life, leadership and business simultaneously is phenomenal, as small changes in each individual area will produce geometric changes in all three areas.

The most important contribution this book can make is to help CEOs challenge their paradigms and make a significant shift to take specific actions to realise their purpose – to be successful a CEO must have a burning desire, a passionate dream and the belief and faith to make it happen by working from the inside out.

I wish you every success in your endeavours.

Adrian Geering
Leveraging your life, leadership and business 100X

1. Starting and Growing a Business

Managing Creativity

How would you manage, lead and grow a range of businesses linked with highly creative non-conformists?

John Chataway

Born: 1953

Education: Elizabeth High School to Year 12, Salisbury College of Advanced Education, Diploma of Teaching.

Career: Secondary teacher; university tutor; freelance editor and cameraman, film industry; editor and cameraman, Co Productions; formed Kojo Productions Pty Ltd in 1992 with business partner Kent Smith.

Personal: John is married with two sons and a stepdaughter. His interests include reading, the cinema and performing arts, and travel. John is also a passionate snow skier.

"Kojo Group is all about **managing creativity**.

There needs to be the right culture to **allow creativity to thrive**

without it going rampant or feral or running out of control. Kojo has developed

a business model that allows creativity to develop

and be expressed **in a commercial business framework**,

hence its success."

Background

John Chataway worked for Kent Smith as a cameraman in the early 90s. As a result of their complementary relationship, experience and skills, John bought into Kent's company in 1992. The company name originated with Kent's wife Jo, who owned a business called Kojo. Already featuring the first letter in each partner's name, it made sense to build the company around it and so Kojo Productions Pty Ltd was formed. Kent and John had aspirations to build a production company that would be the very best in its class. Almost fifteen years later, with a staff of sixty and an annual company turnover of $12 million, they have certainly succeeded.

Products and Services

The company focuses on anything to do with a screen, be it a cinema screen, television screen, computer screen or a mobile phone screen. Each of the eight divisions focuses on some aspect of this market: Kojo Productions produce TV commercials and corporate videos; Oasis Post focuses on post-production editing; Rocket Squad handles animation and special effects; Tracks Adelaide is a post-production sound company; Spirit Films specialises in high-end television commercial production; Kojo Interactive works in multimedia and online web and DVD production; Kojo Pictures develops long-form TV series and feature films; and Kojo Events stages major events for a wide variety of clients.

Growth Trends

The company grew slowly at first and focused on productions only. They subcontracted out all of their post-production work and when their supplier wouldn't grow with them, they started up their own post-production unit. Oasis Post was established as a separate division in 1995 after Kent and John located a key person to run it – Dale Roberts. Dale was a young freelance editor who had the technical and creative skills required to grow the division. This process was then replicated in 1996 with Oasis DVD. In 1998 they established a visual effects company, now called Rocket Squad, after finding a key person to run that with profit share. In 2003, they established Kojo Events in Melbourne, followed by the other divisions mentioned above.

Kojo is able to handle large-scale projects with comparatively low overheads because of its use of subcontractors.

Performance

Overall, the company performance has been good. However, each of these eight divisions are at different stages in their business lifecycle – some are relatively young start-ups and some are ending their life because the market has moved on. This is one of the real challenges facing any company with multiple divisions at differing points on the J-curve. The major issues in businesses like these are capital and cash flow, which is one reason why Kojo introduced additional partners to the business. Cash injections and equity financing helped to reduce Kojo's exposure.

To fast-track their return on investment, Kojo is currently spinning out some intellectual property that has been produced in a joint venture in the digital signage and interactive kiosk areas. In Adelaide, where the majority of the Kojo Group of businesses are based, the issue is the size of the market. However, this has actually been to Kojo's advantage. In larger markets, companies like Kojo have a narrow speciality because of the size of the market. The comparatively smaller size of Adelaide has necessitated Kojo to span a range of projects from low profile, small value projects to high profile, high value projects. Thus, they are well positioned to compete in interstate markets as a broad-based and highly experienced company, well beyond their revenues and staff complement. The other major factor related to performance is the company's culture. "Kojo Group is all about managing creativity. There needs to be the right culture to allow creativity to thrive without it going rampant or running out of control. Kojo has developed a business model that allows creativity to develop and be expressed in a commercial business framework, hence its success."

Structure

A Board comprising five equal partners governs the company, with external partner Steve Wise acting as Chair. At this stage there is no plan to add any non-executive directors. With eight divisions, the structure of the company is quite complex and includes five major areas: Business Development; Film and TV Unit; Kojo Interactive; Kojo Pictures; and Kojo Events. Four of the partners each manage one area, except Kojo Events, which has two General Managers and is located in Melbourne. The divisional structure allows each area to focus on its own specialist area, market and brand. There is also a service company, Kojo Management Services, which provides administration and financial services to the group. Despite the complex structure, the organisation operates in a collegial manner because of the nature of the creative processes and people involved.

Brand

Kojo has had a dual approach to branding. There is a group Kojo brand and a lot of effort is spent broadly promoting this. Then, in the niche markets, each of the eight divisions has built a reputation and brand within that market. For example, Oasis Post has a very good brand in its area but can still leverage off the Kojo brand, and vice versa. Kojo can benefit from Oasis Post's branding in niche markets and can cross-sell Kojo services. It is more expensive to have eight specialist brands but it actually encourages competition between divisions. Kojo is in eight distinct markets that have synergies in terms of the skill sets and technology – a good risk management strategy. If one market is under-performing, the others are able to carry the losses.

Strategic Issues

The most important issues facing Kojo are technology, costs, acquisition and training. With regard to technology, John Chataway believes that, "Technology comes in waves. The surfboard is the intellectual property that we have built to use that technology. The people on the surfboard are our staff. You've got to pick the right surfboard with the right team and the right wave. If you get it wrong, then you don't win. Even if you get a good wave and ride it in, it will eventually peter out. Then you have to turn around and paddle like mad to pick up a new wave of technology".

This creates a number of dilemmas for any organisation in the visual communication industry. The major issue facing the industry is the rate of technological change and the changing delivery and display systems. The big wave now is online delivery. The cost of acquiring and upgrading new technology is always an issue as well as the retention and training of staff who are mainly Generation Y and who are more mobile. There is a real need to offer unique and appealing incentives in order to keep them.

Kojo is involved in global competition and Adelaide is a place to leverage this because of lifestyle advantages and cost advantages. The disadvantages of a comparatively small market are becoming less relevant because of electronic communication. The biggest issue for Kojo is to manage the investment strategies required in each business because of technological change.

INSIGHTS INTO

One of the most important factors is to develop the right culture to allow creativity to develop. This is achieved through employing the right people with the right talent, experience, chemistry and attitude.

Three words are used continuously in Kojo to evaluate and measure everything – generous, savvy and amazing. All staff and everything that is undertaken are measured using these words as a framework.

A great deal of effort goes into maintaining Kojo's culture, which encourages creativity to grow. This is achieved through education, training and learning. It is also achieved by the cross-fertilisation of ideas through creative technology and creative multi-disciplined teams. The company also supplies and sponsors creative events which are in alignment with Kojo's values and direction.

A major focus of the culture is to ensure that every staff member embraces and takes responsibility for the direction in which the company is moving.

Kojo also encourages innovation from every single staff member by empowerment and risk taking through delegated authority. Staff are in teams and are supported by mentors and safety nets who provide encouragement, even in the face of failure. The mentors are also in place to help the company to avoid commercial disasters. This collegial approach fosters learning advancement and creative breakthrough.

WHAT ARE THE SECRETS OF YOUR SUCCESS AS A CEO?

It's management by walking around. It is also my personality, drive and vision, and sharing that vision with staff and colleagues.

What does successful CEO thinking take?

You have to have an absolute belief in your own abilities and the direction you are driving the company and the group. You are the champion of the vision, and every successful project, company, service or product has a champion, and if it doesn't have a champion, it never gets there.

What are the biggest challenges and opportunities of being a great CEO?

Challenges: How to manage upwards as well as downwards.

Opportunities: How to bring everyone along on that dream, both staff and Board. If you don't get both of these right, you've got nothing.

What is the one thing, if it could be done, that would have the greatest impact on you as a CEO?

Better alignment with the Board.

What has been your biggest disappointment as a CEO?

Not realising the importance of managing upwards.

What key decisions have led to your success?

Establishing the model of the eight businesses with the shared services company, with the team of partners co-operating, supporting and helping to refine that.

How many hours a week do you work?

Since getting remarried, about 60. I used to work up to 100 hours a week.

How do you plan?

There are many aspects – a strategic plan for three years. Then a yearly plan, plus budgets, measured monthly, and then a weekly plan.

What are the major factors in your role as a CEO that have helped you, hindered you and blocked change?

Helped you: Support from my fellow partners.

Hindered you: Lack of support from the partners.

Blocked change: Partners.

What part has innovation played in your company?

Innovation is absolutely critical as it is a core value of our company.

What is your succession plan?

Hire from outside.

What is your exit strategy?

To sell my share to the existing younger partners, or others within the group and outside.

What is business success to you?

Running a sustainable business that is generating a profit and will be here for the long term.

What problems do you, as a CEO, talk about on a day-to-day basis?

Relationships between staff, and miscommunications. Also, projects on a day-to-day basis.

What are the issues that you have to deal with in your leadership role as a CEO?

The Board and ongoing conflict resolution between staff.

How has individual and group mentoring helped you?

A lot. The Executive Connection (TEC) has been valuable, and my personal mentor has been invaluable. I remember when I had a crisis how my mentor made himself available at night, outside of working hours, to assist me. I will never forget that.

What changes have you observed in the workplace culture to remain competitive to Generation Y?

It is clear that they are looking for the whole package and they ask, "What's in it for me?" Our motto is to treat them like stars, and this is hard for a lot of baby boomers.

What impact has the business had on your life?

I guess I learned a big lesson when growing the business – I lost my way with my family the first time around. I thought I was doing the right thing by the family by working 80, 90, 100 hours a week. I thought in that way, I was providing for the family. Even though my wife and family were saying, "You're going to lose us", I thought that what I was doing was right, yet in the end I did lose them.

Do you have to sacrifice your own life and family to be successful in business? Any comments?

I used to think you did and now I realise, no.

That balance is fundamental and I realise I'm more effective if I've got that balance right. I had that imbalance for many years while growing the company. I suspect now I would have been much more effective had I got that balance right early. I admire people who have got that right.

How have you capitalised on your business and developed it in an extraordinary way, geometrically?

Using the divisional approach of our company to leverage the company eight times has achieved this.

How has your development as a leader maximised your impact on all of the stakeholders you work with?

My willingness to learn and to listen to advice.

How has your life developed to make you a better person and how have you maximised this?

I work less. I'm more attentive to my family and it's not hard.

Lessons you have Learned as a CEO

Seek as much information and advice as possible, but make up your own mind, and be confident in that decision.

Manage your Board effectively.

Do not have too many J-curves at once.

The importance of systems for intellectual property to save time, and produce consistency.

The value of a good Chief Financial Officer.

Management by Walking Around (MBWA!).

Allow time for creativity.

Learning the lesson that no one knows what's going on. For most of our lives, you assume that everyone else knows what's going on and you're the only one who doesn't. When you realise that none of us knows what's going on, suddenly, we're all even. So everyone's input is valid.

The importance in the value of the brand.

Continual re-evaluation of time spent on tasks. Try and use your time in the most efficient way. Do something trivial because it's a chance to have a "water cooler conversation", without any agenda, to another staff member.

Lead by example and then people will do what you do – for example, putting your own dishes into the dishwasher.

Use multi-divisional structure to grow your company.

Final Word

Believe in yourself, and just do it. There is a story about the American editor who came to work in our office for five months to cut a film, Snow Falling on Cedars. He also edits major television campaigns and he did one for Nike. He asked the Nike staff, "What do we put here?" They replied, "Well, we haven't come up with how we want to finish the slogan. Can you just put in a bit of black until we know what we're going to put at the end of the campaign?" He said, "Okay …" and then he said, "… so, we'll just have to do it, just do it". So, he typed in "Just do it", white on black, and they said, "That's it!"

Questions for Contemplation

As you reflect on John's life, ask yourself:

1. What things could you do differently to better manage upwards, or to manage any of your partners?
2. How could you multiply your business using a divisional model?
3. How could you get more capital to grow your business?
4. What's stopping you from getting balance in your life?

Favorite Book

Funky Business - Talent Makes Capital Dance,

by Jonas Ridderstråle and Kjell Nordström

CONTACT DETAILS

John Chataway

Director of Business Development

Kojo Group Pty Ltd

Email: info@kojogroup.com

Web: www.kojogroup.com

Andrew

Pioneering and Developing a Business from the Initial Spark

What happens when a company is committed to superior customer service?

Andrew Downs

Born: 1963

Education: Woodside Primary and Oakbank Area Schools to Year 11. Electrical Fitting A-Class trade. Post-trade studies: Associate Diploma in Electrical Engineering.

Career: Bridgestone Australia: Electrical Apprentice, Electronic Technician, Maintenance Supervisor, Project Engineer. Established SAGE Automation in 1994.

Personal: Married to Terena. Interests include golf, fitness, travel, and food and wine.

Overview of SAGE Automation

"There is no secret about our very good growth. It was all about **word-of-mouth referrals**. It was about doing a great job, **exceeding expectations**, feeling good about it and **having the same enthusiasm when you talk to the next client.**"

Background

Established in 1994, SAGE Automation was built one job at a time, with the company's success attributable to the passion and enthusiasm Andrew Downs and his team bring to each and every customer. It was that same enthusiasm that led Andrew to initially establish the company, choosing an acronym of nicknames to give the business its memorable title. By listening to its customers and meeting their needs for excellent automation solutions and quality service, SAGE Automation grew rapidly to become a leader in its field. It also began to attract, and continues to attract, excellent staff. In 2000, the company became an unlisted public company with a Board. Four senior managers were invited to purchase shares. The Board now has two non-Executive Directors and five Executive Directors. The company has grown at an average rate of 30% per year over the past 12 years and today has a turnover of approximately $40 million, with 200 staff in both Adelaide and Melbourne. SAGE is now the largest independent systems integrator in Australia. As well as success in the domestic arena, SAGE Automation has become a global player with systems exported to companies in Korea, Germany, Spain, France, USA and Canada, and recently signed its first deal in China.

Products and Services

SAGE Automation supplies electrical engineering services and automation systems to companies in the automotive, infrastructure, manufacturing, food and beverage, wine, water, mining and defence industries. Growth areas for the business are SAGE's service division, mechanical design and consulting services.

SAGE Automation has been involved in a wide range of automation projects nationally and internationally. Coca-Cola Amatil (CCA) had a need for production data from their high-speed plastic bottle and aluminium can lines to support a process improvement initiative. SAGE won the contract and installed their solution on CCA's Northmead packaging line with great success. A national rollout is now underway due to the immense success in Sydney.

Leading German automotive facility supplier Eisenmann awarded SAGE a multi-million dollar contract to supply automation controls for Holden's new general assembly line. SAGE also upgraded the runway lighting systems for the RAAF at various airbases across the country.

In a further sign of its reputation as an "innovation and technology adaptor", SAGE was responsible for the automated traffic re-direction lighting used in the Adelaide Hills Tunnel and the Adelaide Southern Expressway.

Growth Trends

Two major hurdles challenged the company in the early years – lack of business experience and access to finance. The company initially grew out of cash flow and the use of bank overdraft facilities. Debtor finance then assisted further growth, as did funding provided by additional shareholders.

After joining The Executive Connection group (TEC), a CEO leadership development organisation, Andrew was able to network with and learn from the 16 other member CEOs. With access to an experienced Chairman as his mentor and exposure to a range of world-class speakers featured at regular meetings, Andrew was able to gain the necessary advice on how to fund growth and get access to finance. As part of its growth strategy, SAGE Automation developed overseas alliances focused on innovation and benchmarking against the best integrators of processes and automation in the world. SAGE Automation became the only Australian member of the Control System Integrator Association (CSIA) in the USA, an independent association providing world's best practice. SAGE Automation also formed a strategic relationship with US Integrator Advanced Automation Associates, adapting its project management software. Due to this investment in systems, SAGE Automation leap-frogged its competitors and was able to grow at an extraordinary rate.

Performance

The company has performed well in terms of growth of the top line, and the capital value of the business has increased enormously. The bigger issue for SAGE Automation is in the nature of the work that it is attracting. SAGE Automation believes that it is not prudent to win contracts on price alone but instead on innovation, quality, reputation and trust. And even when SAGE is unsuccessful in a tender, the company is, on occasion, called back to finish a job originally awarded to a competitor, or to correct their mistakes. This increases SAGE's value to a client and cements a long-term relationship. SAGE Automation's growing focus on its service division, mechanical design and consulting service (all value-added higher margin business), is contributing to its direction for the future.

Structure

The company structure has gone through a number of transformations over the past 12 years as it has grown. The most recent structure incorporates: a General Manager for SA and one for Victoria; a Chief Financial Officer; a National Engineering Manager; a National Quality Manager; and a National Sales and Marketing Manager for Business Development. Within each region, the goal is to build autonomous businesses with a turnover of $10 million. SAGE Automation believes that this is a good size for customer service, training, account management and accountability, and is similar to the modelling system used by the highly successful company General Electric.

Brand

SAGE's brand has developed as a direct result of its commitment to excellence in automation and quality service. Core values for the basis of its brand include:

*   Customer First – No Matter What

    SAGE Automation's priority is always to do what is right for the customer and to fix problems in a timely way and to the satisfaction of the client.

*   Employ the Right People

    SAGE Automation's fundamental belief is that employing the right people, based on strength of character, will ensure a culture focused on service and quality.

*   Commitment to Excellence and Continuous Improvement

    SAGE Automation is absolutely committed to re-investment in systems and people to reduce repetition, finding better ways, working smarter and challenging the current thinking.

*   Strive to Share Knowledge and Goals

For SAGE, a team approach to goal setting and delivery is crucial. According to Andrew, "It's very hard to set a vision for a company and involve your people if you don't make them directly part of that vision".

*   Work Hard – Play Hard

SAGE Automation is committed to providing opportunities for staff and their families to relax and interact with each other as well as being involved in enjoyable work.

These values have been the reason for the success of the company. Andrew has built a strong staff culture with a strong commitment to quality and customer service. SAGE Automation promotes people from within and there is a philosophy of having a second in command for every leadership role in the company. This ensures that all of the senior managers know the company, know the industry and have chemistry with Andrew and the team. SAGE Automation is currently examining its brand with a view to taking it to the next level to enable growth to $100 million by its focus on value–added services and acquisitions.

Strategic Issues

SAGE currently faces the following strategic issues: repositioning the company with new offerings; attracting and retaining staff because of ongoing skills shortages; continual training and commitment to maintain the culture of the organisation; ongoing refinement of the organisational structure; keeping up-to-date with technology through strategic partners; and achieving profitable growth in new emerging niches.

INSIGHTS INTO
Pioneering and Developing a Business from the Initial Spark

The key to SAGE's growth and success is to be found in the compelling vision and leadership of Andrew Downs. Andrew's passion and enthusiasm for clients (shared by his team) built the business one job at a time through repeat business and referrals. Careful listening to customer needs and providing high quality automation solutions have been accompanied by relentlessly exceptional customer service. The result has been extraordinary growth mainly through word-of-mouth.

Getting and retaining the right staff has been another important factor in SAGE's success. When recruiting, Andrew has always focused on character over experience and technical abilities. Loyal and diligent long-term employees have enabled SAGE to grow to levels beyond Andrew's imagination – and a 95% staff retention rate speaks for itself. Four of Andrew's first hires are now holding senior roles and are shareholders, ensuring ongoing succession and management capacity as the company has grown. As part of an ongoing practice to generate a sense of staff ownership, a number of other senior staff have also been invited to become shareholders in this unlisted public company.

SAGE has a strong commitment to staff training and development. Opportunities for professional growth have encouraged staff satisfaction and retention, creating a self-perpetuating momentum of company growth from staff growth. SAGE also takes a leadership role within the industry in this field. It has a strong apprenticeship and graduate program in place and is developing a new multi-million dollar training centre to ensure staff members and others in the industry have the best facilities at their disposal.

In the early days, Andrew realised that he lacked business knowledge, business experience and access to finance, so he wisely decided to join a business mentoring group that provided peer and one-on-one mentoring. This helped him to grow in knowledge and he learned from others how to run a business and the best ways to finance growth. Andrew also realised that he needed his management team to learn and grow as well. He invested significantly in six key executives to involve them in the same mentoring group. After this exposure to new ideas and expert peer advice, the company implemented a formal annual strategic planning process that has been critical to their success. This process has ensured a clear strategy for selecting the best work to provide profitable growth and has been instrumental in correcting an earlier tendency of growing opportunistically.

Finally, SAGE has grown because of its commitment to, and focus on, policies, systems, procedures and process to maintain consistency, quality and service – all key areas in ensuring duplication and growth.

WHAT ARE THE SECRETS OF YOUR SUCCESS AS A CEO?

I have a lot of passion and I understand the business, which enables me to promote the business and to talk to our people openly about the business. But most importantly it pays to be true to yourself – who you are and what you believe.

What does successful CEO thinking take?

Successful CEOs need to consult their people as regularly as they can. Listen to what your people are telling you, listen to what your customers are telling you, then try to put that together and relate that to your vision. Grab it from inside, grab it from outside and then adjust the vision.

What are the biggest challenges and opportunities of being a great CEO?

Challenges: Surviving some really tough times and coming out the other end stronger.

Opportunities: To grow the business by being a great salesman, team builder and strategist.

What is the one thing, if it could be done, that would have the greatest impact on you as a CEO?

To see the continual growth of our people and having the business function without me.

What has been your biggest disappointment as a CEO?

Having my hard work undermined by circumstances beyond my control.

How do you handle rejection and failure?

I will take it head on. I don't accept it well, like anyone, but I think you have got to look at your options and say, "How can we move forward?" and fix the problem. You can't drive a car looking through your rear vision mirror.

What key decisions have led to your success?

Relentless customer service and pushing that right through the organisation as a core value. Continual improvement, the right people, the right systems and training are all critical decisions. We don't have a business without people and a training culture.

How many hours a week do you work?

I used to work 90 hours per week but now I only work 50 hours per week through the influence of my wife.

How do you plan?

We plan as a Board, and we plan as business groups now. I am thinking and am continually planning and looking at the markets and what is going on.

What are the major factors in your role as a CEO that have helped you, hindered you and blocked change?

Helped you: Being able to develop relationships with people.

Hindered you: Poor personal organisation.

Blocked change: Maintaining the same hunger and drive when things are running smoothly. There can be a risk in good times to rest on your laurels somewhat.

What part has innovation played in your company?

This is a critical area and extremely relevant to our company because of the technology systems and the industries in which we work. Without innovation we wouldn't exist.

How and when have you transitioned your role?

The organisation structure has helped me move from being a hands-on CEO to take on a more strategic role in the organisation.

What is your succession plan?

To appoint a new CEO by promotion within the company and then take up the role of Executive Chairman.

What is your exit strategy?

It is to grow the company's wealth in share value so, when the time comes to execute my exit, it is done with a profitable and positive impact on the business.

What is business success to you?

It is not about money, it's feeling that you have built something – the feeling of accomplishment, continuing to meet new challenges and new people.

What problems do you, as a CEO, talk about on a day-to-day basis?

The problems that get to me come from the managers who need some clarification. They usually come with solutions and need my input related to projects, customers and staff.

What are the issues that you have to deal with in your leadership role as a CEO?

To be an effective leader I feel that I need to be very savvy with the business environment outside of SAGE in relationship to government, financial institutions, lawyers and TEC. I am trying to keep abreast of where it's going and understanding the market through business intelligence.

How do you allow the space and time for creative thinking for yourself and your staff?

I haven't deliberately created space or an opportunity for creative thinking. I think on the run all the time. I find travel to be very good for thinking. I am sure that it would have a great impact on my business and life if I created periods of time that weren't just incidental to travel.

How has individual and group mentoring helped you?

Mentoring has been outstanding for me – the best form of learning you can do is to have one-on-ones with a mentor, if you can talk about experiences. One-on-ones that lack any form of honesty or emotion are terrible. If one-on-ones engage you they can give you so much information.

What changes have you observed in the workplace culture to remain competitive to employ Generation Y?

We have noticed an obsession towards less hours and linking that with lifestyle. It's not about money with these people anymore; it is about quality of life and personal growth.

What impact has the business had on your life?

It's opened up my eyes to everything and broadened my experience. It's endless – other people, businesses, cultures, travel, different organisations; things that I never knew were out there.

Do you have to sacrifice your own life and

family to be successful in business? Any comments?

Yes and I don't really agree with anyone who says you don't. Your sacrifice is to success, but that's my passion in life.

How have you capitalised on your business and developed it in an extraordinary way, geometrically?

Always look at new opportunities. Don't close your mind to new situations or new people. Take time to talk to everyone you come in contact with because something could come from it.

How has your development as a leader maximised your impact on all of the stakeholders you work with?

I lead by example in a lot of cases, particularly in the early days when a job was going bad or something was going wrong. You aren't just a CEO; you are someone who can actually help them.

How has your life developed to make you a better person and how have you maximised this?

By understanding what motivates people, and getting the best from them.

Lessons you have Learned as a CEO

Ensure that everyone is accountable for their actions and that every action leads back to Key Performance Indicators (KPIs) from the business plan.

Always get the best professional advisers to cover your weak points.

Choose a good banking partner.

Benchmark your company by getting information from other businesses that are better than yours.

Establish a Board, as this will provide direct support, stability, accountability and expertise.

Always be continuously improving. Implement the best and latest cost-effective technology to improve what you do.

Grow the culture of your organisation.

Talk to your customer, ask them what they want and do not tell them what they need.

Use debtor financing to help you grow when you have limited access to other capital.

Grow your company by inviting key employees who will be leaders of the company long term to become shareholders.

Grow the organisation through restructuring, training, education and development.

Employ the right people because people are your business. Attract and retain people who are passionate about what they do as this will take your business to the highest levels.

Policies, systems, procedures and processes are key foundations for the success of any company.

Have a compelling vision.

Final Word

Andrew had this SAGEly advice to share:

"Always be prepared to help people be successful. Give them an opportunity to develop. Never diminish people or allow people to depreciate themselves. Always see the potential in people and don't judge a book by its cover."

Questions for Contemplation

Success like Andrew's is possible for you, too. You may like to consider:

1. What similarities are there between Andrew's story and yours?

2. What's stopping you from starting your own business, even if you are currently working for a boss?

3. What are you doing to develop personally? Part of Andrew's secret to success is life-long learning. What actions do you need to take to accelerate your personal development to become the leader and person you were meant to be?

Favorite Book

Good to Great by Jim Collins

Contact Details

Andrew Downs

Managing Director

Email: andrew.downs@sageautomation.com

Web: www.sageautomation.com

Frances

Transitioning From a University-based Organisation to a Commercial Business

How would you change a bureaucratic organisation into a profitable growing company?

Frances Guyett

Born: 1958

Education: Diploma of Education, Melbourne University, 1981; BSc (Hons), Melbourne University, 1986; PhD, Monash University, 1989; MBA, Monash University, 1997; and Graduate of Australian Institute of Company Directors, 2005.

Career: Teacher, Victorian Education Department, 1982-85; Technical Officer, ICI Dulux, 1990-93; Marketing and Product Manager, Bristol-Myers Squibb, 1993-96; Group Business Manager, Sigma Pharmaceuticals Australia, 1996-1998; Cardiovascular Director, GD Searle USA, 1998-2000; Director – Asia Pacific/Latin America, Pharmacia Corporation USA (formally GD Searle), 2000-01; CEO, Medvet Science Pty Ltd, March 2002-July 2006; CEO, RDDT Pty Ltd, Melbourne, August 2006-present.

Personal: In her spare time Frances enjoys spending time with her family, reading, keeping fit, furniture polishing and opera.

"Maintain the passion, stay focused on your vision and act to make it happen."

Background

Frances joined RMIT University's Drug Discovery Technology Pty Ltd (RDDT) as CEO in August 2006. Frances' background consists of 20 years experience in senior executive roles in the pharmaceutical and biotechnology industries both in Australia and overseas (especially in the USA and Japan).

Prior to joining RDDT, Frances was CEO and Director of Medvet Science Pty Ltd for almost five years. Medvet Science is the commercialisation company of the Institute for Medical and Veterinary Science (IMVS) and the Royal Adelaide Hospital (RAH), and provides financial assistance to its shareholders to further support their research capabilities. The company was established in 1985 and, through being continuously profitable, it was able to develop a wide range of businesses as well as allocate its profits to support medical research at IMVS and RAH.

During her time at Medvet, Frances was responsible for a wide range of commercial businesses. This range included: an Intellectual Property (IP) Division (responsible for commercialising IP for over 300 scientists whom undertake innovative research from investigation of basic cell and molecular biology to the development and application of new therapies for the treatment of haematological, prostate and breast cancers, gastrointestinal disorders, arthritis and bone diseases, disorders of the immune system, thoracic and renal disorders and brain injuries); d:tec Australia (Alcohol and Drugs of Abuse Testing); ADME (Alcohol and Drugs of Abuse Testing, Canberra, ACT); Mediflight (medical evacuation and repatriation services); Aushealth (provision of specialised medical services to international patients); FoodLab (food and environmental testing); pre-clinical toxicology testing; manufacturing media and diagnostic products;

GeneMatch (DNA – paternity testing); clinical trials (pathology testing); and the Diagnostic Pathology Laboratory in Alice Springs, Northern Territory.

Under Frances' leadership, Medvet Science improved its financial performance indicators for profitability EBIT (Earnings Before Interest and Tax) (286%), shareholders' equity (85%), return on funds (13%), and she also increased cash holdings by $8.7 million. The profit budget was exceeded in 2004/2005 by 233% ($1.199 million). Frances was also successful in commercialising IP with four spinout companies formed in 2004, and the acquisition of two companies during 2005/2006.

RDDT was founded in 2002 by the School of Medical Sciences, Royal Melbourne Institute of Technology (RMIT) University, as a centre to conduct Good Laboratory Practice (GLP) compliant, pre-clinical safety and toxicology testing for pharmaceuticals, biotechnology, alternative medicines and food additives. Initially called RMIT Drug Development Technology, RDDT was a fee-for-service contract research provider for academic institutions.

RDDT has been recognised by the National Association of Testing Authorities (NATA) as a GLP and an International Organisation for Standardisation (ISO) facility since 2004. The significance of these accreditations ensures that the scientific data RDDT collects is considered of a suitably high standard for acceptance by the Australian Therapeutic Goods Administration (TGA), the US Food and Drug Administration (FDA) and other regulatory authorities.

Currently, RDDT operates from state-of-the-art facilities at RMIT University's Bundoora campus and staff numbers have grown to twenty over the past four years. During 2006, RDDT underwent an expansion strategy with investment from RMIT University and the Victorian State Government to increase its GLP scientific scope, develop enhanced capability and infrastructure for fee-based projects and transition from a government entity to a private company. Currently, the company has revenues in excess of $1 million and will grow to over $5 million by 2010.

The development of a drug consists of a number of phases including target identification, drug identification, lead optimisation, formulation chemistry and pre-clinical testing prior to human clinical trials.

During the pre-clinical testing phase of drug development, an investigational new drug must be extensively evaluated in the laboratory to ensure it is safe and appropriate to administer to humans. During this phase of development, information on the safety and disposition of the drug candidate is obtained. Pre-clinical testing is an expensive and rigorous process. Many biotechnology and pharmaceutical companies outsource this work to expert contract research laboratories (CRLs). There are a number of pre-clinical testing CRLs located in Europe and America but the availability of this expertise in Australia is currently limited, thus providing an opportunity for expansion of this capability locally.

Market Overview

Currently in Australia there are 300 biotechnology companies with an estimated 50% operating in the human health sector. It is estimated that these companies spend approximately $140 million per annum on pre-clinical drug testing overseas – work that could be handled Australia. It should be noted that this market is minute in comparison with the global market, which has an estimated spend of US$41.4 billion annually.

In addition to this market, the application of pre-clinical tests in the product development stage and in other areas (including quality control of biologicals, medical devices and chemicals) will expand the market over the next few years. There are two established GLP accredited pre-clinical testing facilities in Australia and a number of overseas facilities that currently provide pre-clinical services to Australian clients. While these companies are well serviced by their established pre-clinical service providers, there is nevertheless an opportunity for a regulatory compliant Australian facility with a significant cost advantage to capture a segment of this large overseas market.

Products and Services

Australian biotechnology companies generally seek licensing agreements with large pharmaceutical companies prior to commencing Phase III clinical trials. (To ensure product safety, rigorous testing is necessary and standard procedure dictates that clinical trials are undertaken in identifiable stages: Phase I – Human Pharmacology, Phase II – Therapeutic Exploratory, and Phase III – Therapeutic Confirmatory.) Driven by this local market need, RDDT offers a range of services to support the entry of a product into Phase I or II clinical trials – pre-clinical animal testing is a pre-requisite before drugs are approved for testing in human clinical trials. A selection of specialised non-GLP studies is also offered. During the first three years of business, RDDT concentrated on building expertise and historical data on the range of studies offered. To enable the business to offer all studies required to meet international regulatory requirements up to Phase II, RDDT will seek a business partner to contract canine and possibly primate studies.

Strategy

The key business objective of RDDT is to establish a viable Australian-owned, GLP compliant business with a proven track record by 2008. The key technical objective is to provide pre-clinical testing for pharmaceutical and biopharmaceutical products in accordance with regulatory requirements, to support progress into Phase I and II clinical trials. The key market objective is to capture a significant segment of the Australian and New Zealand pre-clinical testing market and a small, but commercially valuable, segment of the potential overseas market.

Structure

RDDT Pty Ltd is 100% owned by RMIT University and was incorporated in early 2007. The CEO, Frances Guyett, reports to a Board that consists of five Directors – three Directors were appointed by RMIT University Council and two are independent Directors. The CEO has four direct reports including: a Research Director, a Quality Manager, a Business Manager and a Finance Officer. RMIT University provides accounting and administration assistance and use of facilities. There are twelve full-time scientific staff, two external veterinary pathology consultants, a veterinary ophthalmology consultant, and casual staff.

Brand

The company is in a growth phase as demonstrated by the following major developments: staff training and development; expansion of the animal house facility; purchase of state-of-the-art scientific instruments; GLP accreditation from the National Association of Testing Authorities; and appointment of key scientific and business personnel.

The positioning of RDDT is focused on quality, timelines, responsiveness to customer needs and local knowledge. The RDDT brand is currently being reviewed and this exercise will be completed in 12 months.

Strategic Issues

The most important issues facing RDDT are: acquiring sufficient funding to support the expansion of technical expertise, capital equipment and scientific scope of services; improving brand awareness for services through increased communication and direct selling to potential clients; implementing and streamlining systems; seeking an external partner; balancing future growth with current financial restraints; and the cost of regulatory compliance. While the company is faced with many issues, it is in its foundation stage and will rapidly grow as its brand is developed through a focused marketing, sales and scientific approach

INSIGHTS INTO

Transitioning from a University-based Organisation to a Commercial Business

One of the major challenges facing Frances Guyett is bringing to reality the transition from a university context to a private company. The university operates in a bureaucratic framework and, as such, has an elongated and slow decision-making process. The key to success is the need to exercise persistence, discretion and patience to allow these processes to take their natural path.

Another challenge is to build the business within the constraints of financial and human resources – usually there is a time lag of six to twelve months between an enquiry and completion of a project. It is quite a balancing act to invest capital to build the internal capability while developing profitable services. It is clear that the CEO has a strong commitment as a leader to build the business through aggressive marketing and promotion, including an ambassadorial role with major stakeholders and potential investors to maintain the current situation and to grow the business. Strategic relations are critical to every business but particularly at this stage of RDDT's growth.

A critical factor related to staff will be to facilitate the profitable growth of the company so that salaries can be paid at commercial rates rather than being tied to salaries paid at university system rates. Another aspect is the need to develop a history of success with regulatory authorities in Europe, Japan, USA and Australia. Currently, the results of pre-clinical trials are sent to clients who submit these to the various authorities for approval. Overseas consultants and overseas testing laboratories presently dominate the marketplace, and there is a lack of client confidence in having studies conducted in Australia. As the company builds its capacity, enhances and develops its brand, and implements a customer relationship management system, it will grow accordingly.

There is no doubt that Frances Guyett's extensive previous experience in developing a similar organisation, and her vision, passion and commitment to outcomes will ensure the necessary growth of RDDT to become a significant player in its industry, both in Australia and internationally.

WHAT ARE THE SECRETS OF YOUR SUCCESS AS A CEO?

Operating a successful, highly technical and regulated business requires in-depth knowledge and industry experience. I believe my secrets of success are my listening skills, leadership ability, business acumen, personality, networking and strategic thinking. I make decisions and do not procrastinate.

What does successful CEO thinking take?

Vision – knowing where you want to head and how to get there.

What are the biggest challenges and opportunities of being a great CEO?

Challenges: Keeping great people.

Opportunities: Ensuring that we become an employer of choice.

What is the one thing, if it could be done, that would have the greatest impact on you as a CEO?

Having the financial resources to employ highly experienced and dedicated staff to whom I could delegate tasks, so I could actually spend more time working on the business for the longer term.

What has been your biggest disappointment as a CEO?

My biggest disappointment as a CEO was in my early years when I delayed implementing a HR decision to ensure that I had the best management team.

What key decisions have led to your success?

My current business is a new biotechnology company spun out of a university environment. Some of the key decisions driving our success include: company structure, Board members, key senior staff and implementing a marketing/sales plan.

How many hours a week do you work?

70-80 hours per week.

How do you plan?

I spend time with my senior team developing an annual plan. Most of my daily planning is conducted during my quiet time at home.

What are the major factors in your role as a CEO that have helped you, hindered you and blocked change?

Helped you: The Executive Connection (TEC) and personal mentoring.

Hindered you: My business is highly technical and regulated, and requires sophisticated scientific equipment and trained staff. Financial resources are a hindrance to employing the experienced staff we need, and to purchasing capital items, but this is always a challenge for any new company.

Blocked change: As this is a new company I am in the process of developing our culture etc.

What part has innovation played in your company?

It's a key factor because we are a biotechnology/scientific company with a limited number of staff. There is a balance between innovation and return on investment, but I am always looking for innovative ideas that can improve my bottom line and increase productivity.

What is your succession plan?

It will be the external appointment of a new CEO with the appropriate experience and drive to build this business.

What is your exit strategy?

When the time is right, my exit strategy will be to look for another opportunity as CEO in a larger company.

What is business success to you?

My profit; making sure we've got a healthy balance sheet and positive cash flow. Also creating a senior management team that can manage this business independently.

What problems do you, as a CEO, talk about on a day-to-day basis?

Funding issues and finding the staff needed to assist in achieving our future goals.

What are the issues that you have to deal with in your leadership role as a CEO?

Currently, the major issues for me as CEO are managing our cash flow and building the business for the future.

How has individual and group mentoring helped you?

Being a member of a CEO mentoring group and having a personal mentor has been absolutely invaluable to me. I can't say enough about the positives. I have gone from a very inexperienced, naïve "wanna-be" to someone who has matured and gone through some very hard learning experiences, and I have come out the other side with a clear vision of success.

How do you allow the space and time for creative thinking for yourself and your staff?

I have implemented some of the techniques that I learned through my mentoring experience – for example, managers' meetings and scheduling time in my diary to brainstorm issues.

What changes have you observed in the workplace culture to remain competitive to employ Generation Y?

In my experience, Generation Y has a different attitude and work ethic. In order to remain competitive I spend more time talking with my staff individually and hosting some social events so that I can get to know them better and understand their needs. In addition, I have been looking at ways to salary package and benchmark our salaries with industry standards.

Do you have to sacrifice your own life and family to be successful in business? Any comments?

I think this question is really a difficult one to answer, but it's related to the nature of the business, the industry, the size of the business, the experience of the CEO versus the inexperience, the age and stage of the person and the age and stage of the business. There are so many factors here that really impact on this question. My answer is probably yes, because most people who have started as small businesses can't survive without doing the hard yards, because you don't have the extra staff capacity or the capital to grow the business – it all has to come from cash flow.

How have you capitalised on your business and developed it in an extraordinary way, geometrically?

Previously, this business focused on providing pre-clinical safety testing services to academic institutions. Now, I am marketing our services nationally and internationally, which has been successful.

How has your development as a leader maximised your impact on all of the stakeholders you work with?

I think it's been a behavioural and attitudinal shift for me over my lifetime. I have taken control and seen the results of what I've implemented as being positive.

How has your life developed to make you a better person and how have you maximised this?

My priorities in life have changed over the last few years and I have gained a greater understanding of who I am and how I operate.

Lessons you have Learned as a CEO

Listening to people. In the past I would normally jump in with solutions right away. I've learned to actually get better over the past years.

Make sure you get a valuation conducted independently when purchasing a company.

Preparing contractual agreements – it's making sure that you don't believe everything a lawyer or a junior lawyer has to say. Really make sure that you get senior, experienced people to review your legal contracts and do it by referrals from other CEOs.

Making your money work for you, whether that's in the right investment portfolio or in new business opportunities.

Most important is to make sure that you've got the right team and that you can trust them.

Act quickly if you have a staff member that you believe does not appear to be performing. Don't procrastinate in making those hard decisions.

Have good corporate governance and transparency at the Board level.

Make sure you get an appropriate mentor or belong to some sort of CEO learning group like TEC to invest in your own development.

Ensure that you grow your business at 15% per year and double it every five years.

Learn the art of growth by acquisition.

Broaden your experience by commencing new product divisions, expanding your business naturally and developing your intellectual property.

Learn to develop new business through spinning out new companies from research.

Learn to float companies on the stock exchange.

Final Word

Create the vision, act on it and make it happen.

Questions for Contemplation

As you reflect on Frances' life, ask yourself:

1. What's next for you?

2. What are you going to change to make sure you don't repeat bad habits or behaviours of the past?

3. How can you grow your business at 15% per annum?

4. How can you influence your Board to practise good governance?

5. What decisions do you need to make to change your life?

Favorite Book

Competitive Advantage Through People, by Jeffrey Pfeffer

Contact Details

Dr Frances Guyett, CEO

RDDT

Email: frances.guyett@rmit.edu.au

Web: www.rddt.com.au

Running a Generation Y Company

How would you start, establish and grow a company with generation Y staff in a competitive industry with a huge monopolistic competitor?

Scott Hicks

Born: 1978

Education: Eyensbury College, South Australia, to Year 12

Career: Managing Director of Adam Internet, established in 1986 as a hobby business and incorporated as a company in 1995.

Personal: Scott is very active and loves not only watching sport but also participating In his free time he enjoys playing basketball, skiing and water-skiing, training at the gym and practising martial arts – in fact, Scott has an impressive three black belts to his name

"Being in the Information Technology (IT) industry, most of our staff are quite young. **Their average age would be less then 25**. We have had to encourage them by making it a fun, young, motivated working place, giving them all the additional things that they want. **They have a fantastic recreation room down on the ninth floor** where they have a TV, Xbox, Coke machine, coffee machine and pinball machines; all of that stuff to keep them occupied – **it's to give them a bit of a break during the day.** We give them a good salary because that is what they are wanting, and let them play with all the new fun toys that we are rolling out with the ADSL 2 and movies-on-demand."

Background

Adam Internet (AI) is a high performance Internet Service Provider (ISP) that has been at the forefront of connecting South Australians to information sources for over twenty years. It was established in 1986 as an Information Technology company. Adam Internet is a fully-owned and operated South Australian business. As the World Wide Web information era cascaded through the business world in the early 1990s, the company responded by developing a broad range of Internet services. In 1995, the company name was changed to Adam Internet to reflect the new strategic direction of the company and since that time has steadily grown, establishing a reputation for providing superior service for Internet connectivity, co-location services and security support tools.

Adam Internet has a large retail and business client base in South Australia of 70,000 users and has built a financially secure company which owns its entire operational network infrastructure, including all the plant, equipment and buildings from which it operates. Adam Internet employs 71 full-time and casual employees through direct employment. However, it indirectly supports the employment of some 150 people through its wholesale network of 13 ISPs located in Adelaide and regional South Australia.

Products and Services

The company provides a wide range of services: wholesale and retail data services including fibre; DSL and wireless solutions; access to their own dedicated fibre loop capable of Gigabit+ connectivity; dial-up capability Australia-wide to support its current customer base and to service clients' mobile data needs when out of the state; wholesale data services to 13 ISPs including dial-up, broadband (ADSL1, ADSL2+) and wireless connectivity solutions; a server hosting farm for co-location customers; and general hosting managed servers and data vault facilities to provide secure server environments, including gaseous fire suppression systems, coded access and video surveillance systems. Video-on-demand, local content and CommunityNet are the specific signatures of their product, enabling Adam Internet to maintain a highly visible presence within Adelaide.

Growth Trends

The company grew slowly at first and as more products and services were added, expanded rapidly to reach a turnover of $21 million by 2007. Their target is a $100 million turnover by 2011. Adam Internet's annual growth now is about 120% per year and is directly related to the development and extension of its products relevant to customer needs.

Performance

Overall, company performance has been very good. This performance is related to the passionate achievement of its vision to provide South Australians with access to information technology related services and to do so with seamless efficiency so that the technology is embraced, not endured.

The company's mission is to be the "one bill" solution for all data, telephony and video-on-demand requirements for South Australians, be that at home, at work or on the move. Adam Internet actively targets customers as individuals, businesses and government entities. It seeks to influence all customers (young and old) who use computers and desire connectivity to the Internet. Their customer base is not predicated on age or income; Adam Internet targets a wide group of customers who are prepared to sacrifice some flexibility for price. Their customers use the Internet for various reasons but tend to be embracers of technology and stereotypically see the Internet as important for their daily interaction. This description is widening as more and more people realise the benefit of connectivity.

Adam Internet has a well-defined set of values that directs the delivery of service to its customers. These include: delivering continuous uptime for customers by providing redundancy (additional capacity) at all layers of its network; offering a reliable 24-hour comprehensive network which automatically reroutes traffic in case of link failure; providing the best in customer service for the business market by operating a highly-regarded technical support centre; offering prompt problem resolution and technical assistance by experienced personnel; maintaining high levels of security; and delivering high speed Internet solutions through "Internet Accelerators".

Delivering on the promise of its vision, mission and values has ensured that AI has continued to grow well and to perform at a high level.

Structure

The company is structured with Scott Hicks as Managing Director, who reports to a small Board made up of an external director (his father) and an external accountant. Scott has five direct reports who manage the company: an Operations Manager; a Sales Manager; a Financial Controller; a Network Operations Manager; and a Marketing Coordinator.

Brand

The brand has developed gradually in line with the number of satisfied users and the range of services. Simple brand recognition has been increased through advertising, which has included television commercials, print, radio, and sponsorships of the Port Adelaide Football Club and the Adelaide 36ers basketball team. Adam Internet relies heavily on word-of-mouth advertising to publicise its resilience, reliability and quality of service.

The company endeavours to be transparent to the customer, so the entire experience "just works". All their advertising is multi-dimensional and cross media and is monitored to determine effectiveness. The use of heavily branded, high-exposure advertising also contributes to Adam Internet's brand recognition. They even have a double-decker bus! This level of advertising in a small region (Adelaide) provides the company with increased consumer awareness of its products, services and reputation. Offices, data centres, vehicles, staff uniforms and customer service are designed to give customers a feeling of quality, speed, professionalism and technology.

Its brand development also relates to the competitive advantage it has achieved through the near-exclusive ADSL2+ capability in South Australia and, in particular, the density of the rollout in the Adelaide area. For a short period of time its product will be unique in that it has gone through four generations of broadband and is now ahead of its competitors. Maintenance of this advantage will be the key to the future and, accordingly, Adam Internet has sought to add a degree of "stickiness" to its product. This includes: attractive set-up cost options that provide contract duration to reduce initial outlay for a consumer; creating a strategic partnership with ReelTime to provide Australia's first video-on-demand capability, delivered via streaming technology to a set-top box; and CommunityNet, a technology that allows customers on the same exchange to share data without additional cost.

Adam Internet has two levels of guarantees to maintain consumer confidence. Firstly, its 30-day tune up allows customers to review their plan within their first 30 days and modify it up or down to suit their requirement – it is then "locked-in" for the remainder of their contract. Secondly, they also provide a "value guarantee" that ensures a customer may review their plan at any time while in contract and upgrade to a plan of equal or greater value for a single cost of $35.

This value guarantee is currently being reviewed to allow a customer to change plans up or down to their initial contracted spend – still at a cost of $35 but with a free plan change every 7 months.

Adam Internet's small geographical spread allows it to offer greater levels of service availability than that of national carriers. The staff are actively involved with the Internet community. They make regular appearances within gaming communities, broadband forums etc. Senior management are involved in radio talkback programs and are guest speakers at many events. All of these activities ensure that AI's brand is being developed and continually communicated to the market place.

Strategic Issues

The most important issues facing Adam Internet are: finding and keeping good customer service staff; maintaining a competitive advantage in an IT company when the rate of change is so great; Telstra's dominance and monopoly in the industry; ensuring that the experience customers have with AI as a one-stop shop is good; training team leaders to be good managers; selecting and retaining the right people; and developing and maintaining the company's unique systems.

INSIGHTS INTO
Running a Generation Y Company

The major issue in attracting and retaining the Y generation in Adam Internet revolves around creating an environment where staff can grow and enjoy what they are doing. Most of the staff at Adam Internet are less than 25 years old – this is because it is a cutting-edge IT company providing work that appeals to the younger generation.

In addition, staff are paid at a high level to encourage strong feelings of career satisfaction. Adam Internet has recently moved into four floors of a multi-storey building in the Adelaide central business district that have been totally refitted to provide a modern working environment for staff.

Adam Internet maintains a distinctive approach in the look, sound and actions of staff; this is documented in considerable detail in the company's guidelines. These policies are not in place to restrict staff individuality, but rather to inject a standard for them to follow which is necessary in such a young and impressionable workforce. The relative "qualification" of an Adam Internet staff member is experience rather than formal education. The nature of its business tends to attract enthusiasts of the technology itself and often this attraction negates the formal qualification needed. Having said that, Adam Internet has staff ranging from 16-year-old school leavers to multi-degree (up to Masters Degree) staff in various departments.

There are six critical success factors that ensure there is a rigorous business focus for the company within a fun environment. These factors include: leadership by the management team through active involvement in customer contact; maintaining clear direction and focus and when sidetracked, quickly re-orientating to regain focus; continually reviewing actions and taking corrective action when necessary; delegating through a system of task assignment and assigning accountability at the lowest level to retain responsibility for completion; having a weekly communication meeting with all available permanent staff (video recorded for review by casual and non-attending staff) to review operational and future issues; and Web demonstrations to provide technical "show and tell" solutions for systems and procedures. All of the above ensures continuity of commitment by staff and the environment to attract new staff with similar values.

WHAT ARE THE SECRETS OF YOUR SUCCESS AS A CEO?

Never create any enemies; always be approachable and be honest.

What does successful CEO thinking take?

I think about what I want and then work out how I am going to get that.

What are the biggest challenges and opportunities of being a great CEO?

Challenge: Looking after the staff – it's a fine balancing act. Having enough time in the day and trying to balance a personal life at the same time.

Opportunities: Growing the business in a competitive environment.

What is the one thing, if it could be done, that would have the greatest impact on you as a CEO?

To continue to mature as a leader by implementing change in the business.

What has been your biggest disappointment as a CEO?

I still take things personally and I guess when people leave, for whatever reason, it is a disappointment.

What key decisions have led to your success?

Focusing on South Australia, investing our money through putting in our own infrastructure so that we have a product that's years ahead of our nearest competitor, and just keeping to the basics. Also, continually providing good value for money and great customer support.

How many hours a week do you work?

That varies a bit, but on average I would try to keep it down to about 50 hours, 5-6 days a week. My fiancé works a lot of shift work, so if she is doing work, sometimes I will work late one night and then we will do something the next night. But I do try to keep weekends to myself.

How do you plan?

I have a very detailed Outlook program that details exactly what I have got to do next. We set KPIs on all of my management staff and have regular weekly and monthly meetings to ensure that those goals are kept.

What are the major factors in your role as a CEO that have helped you, hindered you and blocked change?

Helped you: The major thing that has helped me of late is, definitely, joining The Executive Connection and working with you (Adrian Geering, author of this book).

Hindered you: Taking things personally.

Blocked change: Working with family.

What part has innovation played in your company?

A large part as our company is based on Information Technology that continues to rapidly change.

What is your succession plan?

At the moment I don't have one, as I am relatively young. I am more than capable of leaving this place for 4-5 weeks. The Management Team know exactly what they have got to do and I feel totally comfortable that when I come back, no matter how many weeks I'm away, everything will still be fine.

What is your exit strategy?

Right now I don't have one. We are not currently setting the company up to be sold or anything like that. I would get too bored if I was sitting at home. We plan to run this as a family business long-term.

What is business success to you?

Having a great group of people that trust you. Having a good reputation in the market that you plan. Providing great service to all of our customers.

What problems do you, as a CEO, talk about on a day-to-day basis?

Generally, it's more about day-to-day issues, such as a document that has just been presented to us from an external organisation such as Telstra. Any trouble shooting mostly involves staff not meeting obligations.

What are the issues that you have to deal with in your leadership role as a CEO?

The issues I deal with mostly are with our major suppliers – liaising with them, making sure our relationship is good, catching up with them. Also, meeting new people, and new external contacts in my role as company ambassador.

What impact has the business had on your life?

A huge impact. The business has been everything, or the main thing, in my life for the last 12 years. Everything has revolved around it – my personal life has led into it. But it has also allowed me to do a number of things like travel around the world, meet some fantastic people and better myself because of my role here.

Do you have to sacrifice your own life and family to be successful in business? Any comments?

I did initially. Generally, every single person that has been successful is a workaholic at some point in their life. It is really hard in business to get everything done and to make sure everything is done right. So to an extent, yes. But if you put in the hard work, generally the results pay off and you can step back and enjoy things a bit later on when the company grows.

How has individual and group mentoring helped you?

The TEC group and personal mentoring processes with you have both been fantastic. I have learned more in the last 12 months than I have in probably the last 5 years in business. It's a great sounding board – throwing ideas out, getting advice, and knowing that you are going to get an honest, objective answer rather than someone who is just trying to stroke your ego.

How have you capitalised on your business and developed it in an extraordinary way, geometrically?

The biggest thing that we have done was investing in new technology and getting our own network outlet. We now have a product that no one else has.

How has your development as a leader maximised your impact on all of the stakeholders you work with?

Joining TEC has made a big difference, as has working with you (as my mentor).

How has your life developed to make you a better person and how have you maximised this?

If you compared me with what I was five years ago, I am a totally different person. I have done a number of training sessions to be more outgoing and joined TEC, which has made a big difference. I am now in front of 18 people on almost a monthly basis. I get to do a lot more public speaking, which has given me a lot more confidence.

Lessons you have Learned as a CEO

The most important thing is to always talk to your staff, give them lots of training and give them the information and the tools that they need to get the job done right.

The balance between work and personal life. I make sure that staff take their breaks, go away and do their own stuff.

Putting cash on the line to roll out additional infrastructure that, in turn, puts you ahead of the game, certainly makes a difference.

Keep staying innovative.

Keep employing and investing in new staff in front of the growth curve.

Get the right team in place, particularly the second line.

Keep investing in new technology to make your customers' experience better and your life easier.

Shift into a new facility to improve efficiency, morale and customer and supplier perceptions.

Final Word

Always be truthful; always be honest; set your goals high and strive to achieve them.

Questions for Contemplation

After reading about Scott's success, you may like to ask yourself:

1. How do I need to invest in my life, leadership and business to give me the leverage?

2. How can I achieve goals that I set?

3. What personal development do I need to undertake?

4. How can I improve my balance of life?

Favorite Book

Good to Great by Jim Collins

Contact Details

Scott Hicks

Managing Director

Adam Internet

Email: scott@adam.com.au

Website: www.adam.com.au

Be Remarkable for Something – Building a National Brand in a Profitable Niche

What would you do if you could lose your business through government legislation?

Terri Scheer

Born: 1960

Education: Year 10, Gepps Cross Girls Technical High School; Financial Services Diploma (Broking), 2001; Diploma, Australian Institute of Company Directors, 2006.

Career: Domestic Broking, Alexander Howden Insurance Brokers, 1980-82; Corporate Broking, Jardine Insurance Services, 1982-85; Corporate Broking, Westpac Insurance Services, 1985-87; Corporate Broker, 1987-90 and National Manager Landlord Insurance, 1990-95 MGA Insurance; Terri Scheer Insurance Brokers, 1995-present.

Personal: Terri is married and has one daughter, two stepdaughters, two stepsons, and seven grandchildren. She enjoys travel, cooking, entertaining, gardening, decorating and mentoring.

"The **true measure of a man or woman** is not where they stand at times of comfort and convenience, but where they stand at **times of challenge and controversy.**"

Company Profile

Terri Scheer had worked in the insurance industry for several years when she was asked by her employer to develop the first landlord insurance policy. The product's initial launch and take-up was very successful, however, after returning from maternity leave she found that her employer did not wish to develop the product any further so Terri left and set up her own company. This was a defining moment. Her only asset was a block of land worth $27,000.

In the early days of her business Terri experienced a lot of opposition including: legal and financial pressure from her previous employer; loss of her underwriter; the resignation of a key staff member; and separation from her partner. Despite these setbacks, she persisted and developed the business. The company expanded to every state of Australia and now has offices in New South Wales, Victoria, Queensland and Western Australia. It also services Canberra, Tasmania and the Northern Territory. The New Zealand office, opened in 2004, was sold in October 2006. There are currently 57 staff in five offices including the head office in Adelaide.

Products and Services

Terri Scheer Insurance Brokers (TSIB) is Australia's only specialist landlord insurance broker and currently offers two major products – landlord preferred policy and building insurance. TSIB is a boutique business devoted to providing the best landlord protection insurance and exceptional personal service to property managers. It specifically covers and protects landlords from the range of investment property risks including loss of rental income; malicious damage to property; accidental damage; and legal liability for occurrences on the property that cause death or bodily injury. Previously, owners of rental properties only had access to standard residential building and contents insurance.

Growth Trends

TSIB has enjoyed a remarkable average growth rate of 41% per year and achieved a turnover of $23 million for 2006/07 financial year. Since its establishment, company turnover has increased at an average rate of around $2.3 million per year. TSIB currently holds more than 76,000 policies and is growing at an average rate of 1,800 policies per month.

TSIB has been selected as a preferred supplier by some of Australia's leading real estate groups including: Raine & Horne in South Australia; Ray White; LJ Hooker, First National; and Harcourts.

In 2004, one of the major factors impacting on the company's growth was the Federal Government's Financial Services Reform (FSR) Act. Under the legislation, no insurance broker could use real estate property managers as a distribution channel to sell landlord insurance without expecting real estate agents to go through the onerous process and additional responsibilities of becoming an authorised representative. As a result, TSIB had to contact 76,000 landlords directly rather than 6,500 real estate agents.

A new business model had to be implemented to deal directly with landlords and an estimated investment of $2 million over 12 months was needed.

After many months and long hard hours with lawyers and the team, a new business model, "Scheer Simplicity" was developed and implemented. This enabled property management customers to refer TSIB financial services to their landlords within tight guidelines that would ensure they were legally compliant. Some property managers remained fearful of being sued by landlords and of being punished by the Australian Securities and Investments Commission (ASIC) if they inadvertently breached the requirements of the FSR Act. As the fear set in, the number of landlords with insurance through TSIB fell by 51% and the saleable value of the business fell by $9 million. It also left landlords and property managers exposed to significant legal and financial risk.

Showing great courage and determination, Terri Scheer attacked the issue with two strategies – industry education and consultation, and political lobbying. As a result, ASIC announced on 27 October 2005, some 18 months later, that it would grant relief to licensees from some requirements for distribution of general insurance products. Property managers could once again fulfil their duty of care to landlords.

In 2006 Terri implemented "Project 007 Never Say Never" – a staff incentive program for achieving 100,000 current policies by June 30, 2008. Terri's aim is to build the business and reward trust and performance among her staff. The company is expecting sustainable growth to continue. It is also developing several new products including an insurance policy for holiday rental properties, a business insurance pack and motor vehicle insurance specifically designed for real estate agents.

Performance

The company's performance has been extraordinary in terms of its growth rate and profitability. Since its establishment in 1995, turnover has grown at an average rate of 41% per year at both the top and bottom end. In 2003/2004 the turnover reached $18.4 million from $8 million in 2001/2002. The company's profitability as a percentage of sales has improved consistently.

TSIB has achieved much external recognition. In 2001, it was named Australia's seventieth fastest-growing company in the BRW Fast 100 companies list and Terri Scheer was a finalist in the Ernst and Young

Entrepreneur of the Year. In 2002, the company was the first to be granted an Australian Financial Services license under the FSR Act. In 2004, TSIB was named Telstra South Australian Small Business of the Year. In 2006, Terri Scheer was ranked ninth in BRW's list of Top 50 female entrepreneurs in Australia and also won both the Westpac Business Owners and Australian Government Innovation Awards which led to winning the Telstra South Australian Business Woman of the Year.

Above all Terri has provided visionary leadership to her company team through clear direction. As a company ambassador she has developed key relationships with clients and the real estate industry.

Structure

The company has a General Manager who focuses on business services and a Marketing and Operations Manager who oversees the operations and marketing with support from a National Sales Manager. There is an Executive Management team of four in the Adelaide head office and a senior representative in each state office.

Brand

The brand is highly recognised and associated with innovative landlord insurance consistently delivered with the best service and support. The company-wide strategy is a single focus on achieving the goal of 100,000 policies by June 30 2008. This single focus, supported by a highly trained staff and customised software, has allowed the company to achieve a market share of $23 million in 2006/07, out of an estimated $80 million in gross premium annually in the sector – 36% of the market. When the company achieves its "007" target of 100,000 policies, its market share may increase to 42%.

Development of the brand has been related to three major factors: developing a quality, relevant product; being committed to superior customer service; and focusing on loyalty to property managers.

- Developing a quality, relevant product

When the landlord insurance product was released by TSIB, it was the most comprehensive product of its kind in Australia. The quality far surpassed competitor products leading to high demand from landlords and property managers and continuing loyalty.

- Superior customer service and support

TSIB recognised that insurance was only one aspect of a property manager's responsibilities to landlords, and simplified the process by offering: personal training; phone inquiry service; national service network and risk management processes; settling 95% of claims within 14 days; pursuing offending tenants in every claim; monitoring renewal dates; and strongly supporting the real estate industry. This approach has resulted in customer retention of 99.5%.

- Loyalty to property managers

Policies are only offered to landlords who have appointed property managers. This close relationship with property managers ensures the ongoing offer of the product to new landlords.

Strategic Issues

Strategic issues for TSIB include: continued legislative reform; excess of capacity within the insurance industry; new competitors; continued interest rate rises; housing shortage; changes to superannuation legislation; and the potential downturn from housing investment.

INSIGHTS INTO

Building a National Brand in a Profitable Niche

Terri Scheer has defied the odds. She focused on one product, building a national brand, and dominating a niche. Why has she been so successful?

1. Terri Scheer was first to design a specialist product for the national market of landlords. Owners of professionally managed rental properties previously had no access to specialised insurance that would protect them from loss of rental income from tenants who caused malicious damage.

2. The Landlord Preferred Policy was the most comprehensive landlord insurance product in Australia providing a full range of cover for landlords.

3. The product stood apart from other standard insurance policies which either did not cover the risks associated with rental properties, or had large excesses.

4. The product remains a leader through ongoing innovation. For example, it now covers landlords for tax audit expenses, something that no other policy does.

5. TSIB is committed to pursuing tenants in every claim.

6. Property managers have access to a product that protects their interests, as well as those of their landlord customers, in cases of legal action by a tenant.

TSIB created a new industry altogether focusing solely on landlord insurance products, estimated to be worth $80 million per year. Herein lies the secret of Terri's success – a narrow focus on a quality, relevant product and superior customer service. Many companies, in contrast, have many products and the Pareto principle applies: 80% of the success comes from 20% of the products. In TSIB, a 100% rule applies. Also, the company has become famous for something. TSIB is synonymous with landlord insurance. So the secret is to be remarkable for something. The reality now is that TSIB can sell the concept as a franchise overseas and introduce a full suite of targeted products for both landlords and real estate agents while preserving this central focus.

Operating as a CEO

WHAT ARE THE SECRETS OF YOUR SUCCESS AS A CEO?

Be prepared to do and go wherever you have to, to make a change, and to have all the hardest problems land on your desk. Do what your instinct tells you is the right thing to do.

Be a good listener, be innovative, and constantly develop your own professional skills. Monitor the quality of your self-talk. At all times, promote the development of the people you work with. Protect your reputation at all costs and develop strong relationships with people of influence within your environment.

What does successful CEO thinking take?

You have to overcome your own fears, believe that you can rise to any challenge, and be a good visualiser.

What are the biggest challenges and opportunities of being a great CEO?

Challenges: Maintaining your energy and passion.

Opportunities: Having a hand in other people developing; and creating a name for yourself that stands for something worthwhile.

What is the one thing, if it could be done, that would have the greatest impact on you as a CEO?

To be able to develop clones.

What has been your biggest disappointment as a CEO?

Employees who disrespect the company and their teammates.

What key decisions have led to your success?

Investing in my own personal and professional development, and particularly my mentor.

How many hours a week do you work?

60 at work; but three times that when you include thinking time.

How do you plan?

There are certain non-negotiables in the diary – my physical fitness, my TEC meetings and my one-on-ones. I try to keep one day a week for meetings. I plan my travel well so that I maximise family time. As best as I possibly can, I don't physically work in the business on the weekends.

What are the major factors in your role as a CEO that have helped you, hindered you and blocked change?

Helped you: Having a mentor and coach, especially having had the same person consistently.

Hindered you: Fear of failure; being the underdog; and the loneliness of the CEO role.

Blocked change: Lacking the physical energy to do it myself when I haven't had the resources around me; and the regulatory environment outside of my control.

What part has innovation played in your company?

It's been everything. It started us, it's maintained us and it continues to keep us ahead of the pack.

How and when have you transitioned your role?

Once I had two strong managers on board, I transitioned into a CEO from a Managing Director.

What is your succession plan?

I have a practical succession plan in place. If anything happens to me I have an heir appointed from an external company who knows the business very well. I have it documented and insured. If he doesn't take it up, then the General Manager will.

What is your exit strategy?

Sell the business.

What is business success to you?

Being recognised in the community as standing for something that is of strong reputation and quality, and having had a hand in the development of a huge number of people along the way.

What problems do you, as a CEO, talk about on a day-to-day basis?

Impact of competitors and key indicators like interest rates and property movement.

What are the issues that you have to deal with in your leadership role as a CEO?

Maintaining my image personally because I lead by example.

How has individual and group mentoring helped you?

It provided benchmarking and access to a wider range of experience and a greater appreciation of what we're achieving as a company. Mentoring can really help me to confront issues, and address problems as well as encouraging me to grow to the next level.

What changes have you observed in the workplace culture to remain competitive to employ Generation Y?

Training is important as well as having up-to-the-minute technology. Also, being willing to have a young company attitude; to be innovative and not too conservative.

What impact has the business had on your life?

At times it's hard to control, but the harder I work the luckier I get.

Do you have to sacrifice your own life and family to be successful in business? Any comments?

No, not if you put them first. Put them first and then everything else happens around them.

How have you capitalised on your business and developed it in an extraordinary way, geometrically?

I have grown the business opportunistically and multiplied it as much as I could, at high rates of growth, adhered to its core values and never compromised.

How has your development as a leader maximised your impact on all of the stakeholders you work with?

By being bold and courageous. You've got to emanate what you want.

How has your life developed to make you a better person and how have you maximised this?

I've learned the value of being open to any possibility or opportunity, and being willing to challenge the established norms. Avoid assumptions; challenge everything.

Lessons you have Learned as a CEO

Software will always cost you one hundred times more than they originally quote and take 10 times longer to develop.

Never underestimate your competitors or the ability of legislation to stuff up a good business.

Clients are everything. Ensure that your company is easy to do business with. Help clients with their need to be successful with their own clients.

Never underestimate the power of the whole team being fully informed about the company changes and inviting their involvement.

Get rid of non-performers quickly.

Your people will watch and take in everything you do and see to a far greater degree than you think they do. They don't miss a trick.

Implement a regular price rise in your products.

Be prepared to take risks rather than run away, be prepared to stay and fight the impact of barriers to your business, such as legislation.

Prioritise your own fitness, health and wellbeing.

Take time out for yourself when necessary.

Recognise defining moments in your career as a CEO.

Teach yourself that you can overcome your fear and you can go places you haven't been trained to go. Also you can make a difference if you try and are willing to put yourself out there.

Final Word

It has everything to do with not being afraid. Put your background behind you; all things are ready if our minds be so. If you know that what needs to be done is going to save your business and save the people for whom you're responsible, then be prepared to do it; even when that means overcoming a lifelong fear of failure, inadequacy, and poor education, which makes you question yourself and worry you'll look like an idiot.

Questions for Contemplation

As you reflect on Terri's life ask yourself:

1. If you really want to make a difference, are you prepared to give everything you've got to that cause, despite your background?

2. When is enough enough?

3. What is blocking you from doing "the impossible?"

4. What would you do if you weren't afraid?

Favorite Book

Inspirational Leadership, by Richard Olivier

Contact Details

Terri Scheer, CEO

Terri Scheer Insurance Brokers

Email: terri@terrischeer.com.au

Website: www.terrischeer.com.au

2. Developing and Maturing a Business

Doing the Right Things for the Right Reasons – Building the Best Credit Union in Australia

How would you run an organisation to serve its members and give to the community?

Greg Connor

Born: 1956

Education: Year 12, Woodville High School; Bachelor of Education, Adelaide College of Advanced Education; Graduate Diploma, Business Administration, South Australian Institute of Technology

Career: Training Manager, John Martin & Co. Ltd, 1977-81; Personnel and Industrial Relations Officer, ICI, 1981-84; Chief Human Resource (HR) Manager, Beneficial Finance, 1985-91; Principal HR Consultant, State Bank/Bank SA, 1991-95; Chief Manager Operations, Bank SA, 1995-2000; and CEO of Savings & Loans, 2000-present

Personal: Family and friends, and participating in and watching sport.

"Do the right things for the right reasons. If you focus on your values and excellence and take action in alignment with these values, then anything is possible. All companies make plans; great companies bring them to life."

Background

In 1999, Greg Connor was working in a strategic position with Bank SA. He was responsible for overseeing all metropolitan branches, for helping the new owner, St George Bank, with corporate human resources services and for leading the bank's Y2K project in South Australia.

A colleague, who was CEO of another organisation, saw an advertisement for the role of CEO of Savings and Loans Credit Unions (S&L CU) and convinced Greg to apply. At first Greg hesitated: "I was really enjoying my role at Bank SA. However, it was an opportunity to actually run my own ship and this was part of what I wanted to do; being in South Australia was important to me. Also, the bank was increasingly becoming Sydney based and I could see myself being inextricably drawn over there". So Greg successfully applied for the job, became CEO and began leading an organisation that was not as deep as his former one, but was significantly broader, and with its own Board.

Products and Services

S&L CU is similar to a retail bank. It provides a range of lending products, including home loans and personal loans, as well as credit card services. It has all the usual deposit structures and deposit products, ranging from online at-call deposits through to fixed deposits. S&L CU also offers the standard face-to-face transaction options through a branch network and provides member access through an ATM network, agencies and Internet banking. Ancillary products include financial planning and insurance.

Growth Trends

S&L CU has grown at a steady rate of 15-20%, compounding each year. When Greg joined S&L CU in 2000, it had $650 million in assets. Now, under Greg's leadership, it has grown organically to $2 billion in assets, with 540 staff and over 170,000 members, making it the third largest credit union in Australia.

Performance

S&L CU has performed very well, particularly in recent times. In the 2005/2006 financial year growth remained strong, with the company achieving an after-tax profit of $14.92 million and assets above $1.8 billion. Personal loans were solid and exceeded $107 million during this period.

The performance in other measures has also been outstanding. The latest staff satisfaction survey placed S&L CU in the highest category for financial institutions, with over 500 staff recording a satisfaction level of 83%. During the past seven years, staff turnover has dropped from 30% to 11% and staff satisfaction has risen from percentages in the mid-50s to the mid-80s. Staff continue to provide excellent service to members, which is reflected in the results of a recent member survey. This survey reported a 90% customer service satisfaction rating, placing S&L CU in the top quartile for all financial institutions.

S&L CU has also received recognition for its excellent products and services by being awarded Personal Lender of the Year in 2006, for the second year in succession. It was also awarded Credit Union of the Year in 2006, an accolade it has achieved for the past four out of five years. In addition, an Employer of Choice for Women citation was received from the Equal Opportunity for Women in the Workplace Agency.

In the last financial year, S&L CU entered the Corporate Responsibility Index (CRI), a tool developed by the St James Ethics Centre and audited by Ernst & Young to measure the corporate social responsibility of an organisation. The organisation performed exceptionally well, achieving a Silver Star level and receiving "best newcomer" award – appropriate recognition of the time and effort that has been invested into social and environmental responsibility.

The organisation's seven-year partnership with the Women's and Children's Hospital (Adelaide) reached a pinnacle in May 2006 with the opening of the Savings & Loans Emergency Department. A total of $2.5 million was raised for this redevelopment through the S&L CU Women's and Children's Hospital Visa card, an award-winning community partnership that saw a percentage of each purchase made with the Visa card donated to the hospital.

The performance of S&L CU is not seen by management in purely monetary terms but is a reflection of its focus on members and of finding ways to give something back to the communities in which members live and work.

Structure

S&L CU is a mutual organisation that is owned by the 170,000 members who each purchase a $2 share giving them the right to vote and participate in the running of the company as a shareholder. They elect the Board, which consists of eight directors.

The CEO has seven direct reports who are responsible for the functional areas of the organisation including: the General Manager, Distribution, who looks after all the branches and the call centre; the General Manager, Marketing, who looks after a $4 million marketing budget; the Chief Financial Officer, who focuses on finance; the Deputy CEO, who looks after strategy and business development; the General Manager, Business Services and Technology, who runs the engine room from a people and IT point of view; the Executive Manager, Audit and Risk; and the General Manager, People, Culture and Sustainability. The company's structure well supports its strategies and goals.

Brand

The S&L CU brand is gaining increasing recognition but is still well behind that of other financial institutions, primarily because of its size – for example, the Commonwealth Bank's larger size reflected a profit last financial year of $2 billion, the same size as S&L CU! Banking is built around two things – money and people, so S&L CU has strategically followed a service/profit chain model to empower, train and retain great people. This develops a brand that is recognised as providing well-trained and happy staff who give great service – a critical factor in growing brand recognition.

In conjunction with the service/profit focus, the organisation has just released a new simplified vision, refining its values and developing a framework for S&L CU to be a leading provider of financial services in Australia. The new vision is to be the best member-owned financial institution for everyday Australians and this will be the focus of all of its internal and external activities in developing its brand. S&L CU's core values are trust, mutual respect and integrity within the context of excellence, financial soundness and social responsibility. The organisation has decided on six strategic pathways to deliver their new vision including: an increased understanding of members' needs; enhanced member value; focused, organic growth through geographic expansion, alliances, mergers and acquisitions; being easy to deal with; corporate financial responsibility at individual, local, national and international levels; and environmental responsibility.

Strategic Issues

The most important issues facing S&L CU today are increased competition, increased regulations, changing member needs, and implementation of new technology. Costs will increase because of the growing complexity required to comply with the law. The need to attract new members and encourage them to buy services means investing considerable money in researching what members want and what causes them to join, stay and buy the products and services offered. The needs to invest in new technology, and to select the right technology, are important issues. S&L CU has invested in a company called Data Action, which develops software and IT capabilities for many credit unions. As a result, they have been able to significantly leverage off this because of the shared investment risk and the lower cost of processing for shareholders.

S&L CU has been successful because of its culture and leadership. As Greg Connor says, "When I joined S&L CU as its CEO, it was a good organisation just waiting for someone to take it to be a great organisation."

Apart from the obvious need to be strategic, to work with the Board and represent the company, Greg's contribution as a leader has been to build his team and to develop the culture of the organisation. Initially, this involved getting his executive team to understand that S&L CU could be a big organisation with controlled profit and growth.

The other challenge Greg faced was continuing to grow the workplace culture as more people came into the organisation. "We get great people, empower them, train them, and keep them happy – then they'll give great service. This means that we will get more business incrementally than anyone else." So, success for S&L CU comes through its people – that is, staff delivering the results through great service to members. Not only this, but it's the way in which Greg and his team have involved their people in the way they do business. It's about the staff owning the decisions, growing with the decisions and making the decisions happen.

However, this means staff must be prepared to "handle tough love at a meeting, in terms of being able to have a rigorous debate about a business issue within the executive team, getting to the right decision for the organisation, then everybody walking away knowing it's not personal. Nobody feels affronted by that sort of process. That's a hard thing to manage and to get because sometimes people feel their project is their baby and somebody else is calling their baby ugly!"

Greg's leadership genius extends to knowing when to coach staff to do new things, when to give them scope to create new things themselves, and when to challenge them on the occasions that they haven't quite got it right. He leads from behind to help them grow and develop as leaders – a big factor in explaining the success of S&L CU in their competitive markets.

WHAT ARE THE SECRETS OF YOUR SUCCESS AS A CEO?

It's about knowing yourself and knowing about people – understanding the power you wield. It's having a business sense which allows you to ask the hard questions at the right times and having the managerial sense to shut up when you should!

What does successful CEO thinking take?

As a CEO, you need to think on a number of levels at different times. You have to "strategic think", which is determining where you want the company to be in three to five years. You have to "Board think", which is about working with your Board to get the best for the organisation, short and long term. You have to "operational think", which is running the business day-to-day. And you need to "people think" about growing and developing people. A successful CEO knows which thought process to use during any business cycle.

What are the biggest challenges and opportunities of being a great CEO?

Challenges: It's all the things we've just spoken about, but with a bit of luck added to it. A great CEO needs longevity, so it's about being able to refresh and not being stale; it's not about doing things "just because it works", because if you do, you risk having the same results over and over, with no change and no progress. The challenge is in knowing when to make those hard or different decisions – to sense the right timing.

Opportunities: If you can get the timing right, then you can be with a company for 20 years and never have any year twice. The company would probably say that if you were there that long and had that cycle right, you'd actually be working for four different companies.

What is the one thing, if it could be done, that would have the greatest impact on you as a CEO?

What every CEO in financial services has endeavoured to do, and has never been able to do, is to make banking easy, and that's one of our strategic projects. If we can make it easy, in terms of being easy to deal with, then we would have the silver bullet. But it's a bit like the legend of the Sisyphus. Sisyphus is a mythical beast that rolls a rock up a hill and just wants to get it to the top and then his life will be complete. He never, ever gets it to the top. It rolls back down – and he has to start all over again. There are people cleverer, richer, greater, and who have research departments bigger than my whole company, who are trying to find the elusive "silver bullet" – and they haven't got it right yet.

What has been your biggest disappointment as a CEO?

At the moment, it would be that we haven't been successful in a merger with another large credit union.

What key decisions have led to your success?

I think that the development of Savings & Loans has been a gradual process. One of the major ones was our growth strategy in 2001, which we are still following and that's exactly as it is in the strategic plan.

How many hours a week do you work?

On average, between 50 and 60 hours.

How do you plan?

The organisation has a 3-5 year strategic plan, which is "operationalised" into a 12-month budget and reported on monthly to our Board. But I plan my days on a daily basis, as well as weekly, monthly and yearly to ensure that all important priorities are allocated time.

What are the major factors in your role as a CEO that have helped you, hindered you and blocked change?

Helped you: When I got here, there was a wonderful culture sitting here which just needed to be developed and grown.

Hindered you: The lack of brand presence of credit unions in the marketplace.

Blocked change: The financial one is about our ability and size. We couldn't grow as quickly as I would have liked in some areas in terms of putting in branches and exploiting new opportunities.

What part has innovation played in your company?

Innovation has played a great part in that we need to be creative, slick and quick to make a mark against the bigger players. We encourage innovation from the tellers through to the Board.

What is your succession plan?

A smart CEO has a team better than him or her underneath them, so my succession plan is to develop to a point where there might be one or two people who could take my place from within the organisation. We're not there yet, but we're getting close.

What is your exit strategy?

I think I'm too young to have one of those!

What is business success to you?

It would be leaving an organisation in significantly better shape than when you arrived. That when you leave, the business doesn't miss a beat.

What problems do you, as a CEO, talk about on a day-to-day basis?

People problems, regulatory problems and business problems in terms of competitors and what we're doing in terms of our sales.

What are the issues that you have to deal with in your leadership role as a CEO?

Ultimately, they are about dealings with the Board, dealing with major suppliers and dealing with regulators. I have the delegated responsibility to dismiss anybody in this place from the Board downwards; the ultimate issue I would face would be the need to sack someone or a number of people.

How has individual and group mentoring helped you?

It's lonely at the top, so it's great to have people, either as a group or individually, with whom you can throw ideas or concerns around without fear or favour. It makes you a better CEO and a better person.

What changes have you observed in the workplace culture to remain competitive to employ Generation Y?

They are the "now" generation, so one of the things that we deliberately do is to have innovation groups and groups working on issues or challenges which are cross-functional. We have younger people working on them as they love working on projects as well as their own jobs, and so by getting them involved and getting their ideas, you're keeping them alive, and that means they are keen to stay with us.

What impact has the business had on your life?

It's been both a positive and a negative. It does allow you to do some things that normally would be out of one's reach, but on occasion it also can have very much a negative impact on the time and the quality of life that you spend with your family.

Do you have to sacrifice your own life and family to be successful in business? Any comments?

Well, I'm in a mentoring group and once a year everybody looks at their goals in life and, invariably, one of the common goals and concerns is the work/life balance. So, the answer would be "Yes, I have" and I'm yet to meet the person who has been super-successful in a business and not had to make some sort of sacrifice.

How have you capitalised on your business and developed it in an extraordinary way, geometrically?

We have had consistent, double-digit growth and we've capitalised on that by leveraging off the people that sit here. Somebody had to come along and realise this was a great organisation. They didn't have to create it; they just had to grow it.

How has your development as a leader maximised your impact on all of the stakeholders you work with?

I think that I have grown in my strategic ability and also my ability to manage people and help them achieve their goals.

How has your life developed to make you a better person and how have you maximised this?

I grew up in the toughest part of Port Adelaide and, in the early days, I went through the school of hard knocks. Being able to come from humble beginnings and understanding the value of the goal and the value of people means that I'm a better manager because I understand what drives people, motivates them and grows them.

Regarding the development of your company, your leadership skills and your life, how have you used growth in these areas to maximise your impact on the community?

Primarily, I joined a credit union that is a mutual organisation that seeks to maximise its impact within the community as a strategic intent. This has been a great vehicle for me to impact and influence the community.

Lessons you have Learned as a CEO

People really are your most valuable resource.

It really is lonely at the top.

You need to understand the invisible power that you wield as CEO.

Sometimes in business there is no right answer.

It can be okay to make mistakes; just don't make them twice.

Don't believe everything you read in books.

Nobody knows whether marketing really works.

The true way to measure an organisation is through a balanced scorecard (you need to consider the financial, people and community aspects).

When you are a comfortable, medium-size fish in a big pond and have the opportunity to become a big fish in a medium pond, then take it and grow.

When you make a major change (which for me was moving from an advisory role in HR to Chief Manager running the branches of Bank SA), it may be very scary for a while. However, it may also be the best decision that you have ever made because it allows you to grow.

If you consistently do the right things for the right reasons, then success will flow.

When in doubt, refer to the first point.

Final Word

A smart person working alone can do good things; a clever person working with people can do great things.

Questions for Contemplation

As you reflect on Greg's life, ask yourself:

1. How good would you feel if your peers voted you as CEO of the Year, but your kid said that you were a lousy mum or dad?

2. How much do you contribute to the community?

3. How are you empowering your team?

4. What is the next opportunity you must take?

Favorite Book

Sacred Cows Make the Best Burgers, by Robert J. Kriegel

Contact Details

Greg Connor, CEO

Savings & Loans Credit Union

Email: gconnor@savingsloans.com.au

Web: www.savingsloans.com.au

Building Your People to Build Your Business

How can you use your business and life to change the world?

Bob Day AO

Born: 1952

Education: Gilles Plains High School to Year 11; Science Technician's Certificate, South Australian Institute of Technology.

Career: Laboratory Technician, South Australian Government Highways Department, 1969-75; Plumber, Day & Night Plumbing, 1975-82; Builder and Director, Homestead Homes, 1982-96; and CEO, Home Australia Group, 1996-present.

Personal: Married with three children, Bob sings and plays the guitar and has his own band called Green River. He also enjoys stamp collecting, is active in federal politics and is a member of the Houghton Uniting Church.

"Consider the postage stamp – its usefulness lies in its ability to stick to one thing until it gets to where it has to go."

Company Profile

Bob Day started his working life in the public service before discovering there was more to life than just counting down the days until retirement. He fell into the home building industry in 1975 when an old school friend, who had become a plumber, needed some help on a building site. Bob decided to attend night school to get his plumber's ticket and builder's registration, and subsequently went into the plumbing business. In 1982, Bob formed Homestead Homes and built his first house. The company grew rapidly. By 1995 the company had achieved a turnover of $50 million and was building about 1,000 houses per year.

In 1996, Home Australia Group was formed from the base of Homestead Homes and the company acquired a number of interstate building companies including: Collier Homes, Western Australia in 1996; Newstart Homes, Queensland in 2000; Ashford Homes (a start-up), Victoria in 2002; and Huxley Homes, New South Wales in 2003. The group has combined sales of about $200 million in five locations. It employs 200 staff and many sub-contractors in the various building trades.

Product and Services

Home Australia focuses exclusively on home building, with design and construction based on a comprehensive range of single and double storey houses, all presented in attractive catalogues for each company. All designs are standard but can be tailored for each customer's needs.

Growth Trends

After reaching $50 million and building over 1,000 houses in South Australia, Bob Day realised that with the limitations of the South Australian market he needed to grow interstate. Additionally, this interstate expansion complemented his interests in the Housing Industry Association and other community activities. The company acquired Collier Homes in Western Australia in 1996 and achieved combined sales of $78.5 million by 2000. With the acquisition of Newstart Homes in Queensland in 2000 and the start-up of Ashford Homes in Victoria in 2002, sales topped $86.5 million in 2002. When Huxley Homes in New South Wales was acquired in 2003, sales grew to $132 million. Since then, as the acquisitions have been consolidated, growth has continued and sales are in excess of $200 million annually.

Performance

The company's growth in sales and profitability has been outstanding. South Australia and Western Australia have led the way with Queensland and New South Wales following. The company has achieved its growth through well-established brand names, sales training systems (using the Sales Doctor® program), a network of display homes, community involvement and hiring good management and staff.

This focus on having a good organisational structure and excellent systems has been critical to their success. In each of the five companies, there is a General Manager (GM) who has five direct reports – an Estimating Manager (pricing), a Sales Manager (selling), an Administration Manager (processing through shire councils), a Construction Manager (building) and a Finance Manager (money in, money out). Each of these managers reports to the General Manager and ensures that good tight systems are maintained for high performance.

The performance of Home Australia is also related to the contribution of Bob Day to the Australian community. His strong interest in youth unemployment, homelessness, urban planning, federalism and industrial relations has been reflected in a wide range of appointments that include:

National President of the Housing Industry Association;

Founder of Independent Contractors of Australia;

Director of The Centre for Independent Studies;

Member of the National Work for the Dole Advisory Committee;

Chairman of North East Vocational College; and

Founder of www.nationbuild.com.

In 1991, he was named Westpac Young Executive of the Year and in 1993, he won Marketer of the Year. On Australia Day 2003, he was appointed an Officer of the Order of Australia for service to the housing industry, to social welfare – particularly housing the homeless – and to the community. Later that same year he was awarded the Centenary of Federation medal for service to housing and charity. In 2005, he was awarded the Pride of Australia medal for "Community Spirit", for restoring the village of Houghton and creating the Soldiers Memorial Walk and Remembrance Wall. He has recently been endorsed by the Liberal Party as a candidate for the federal electorate of Makin in South Australia.

Since 1990, Bob Day has been a member of a mentoring group that has assisted in his development as a leader. This group has been instrumental in helping him implement business excellence in management, sales and marketing, finance, and information technology, as well as in recruiting, training, inspiring and retaining high calibre people.

Structure

Home Australia operates as a group with five separate companies, each of which is run by a General Manager. Bob Day is Managing Director and CEO and his long-time business partner and former school friend acts as Executive Director and assists him in several areas, particularly with purchasing from suppliers. There is a Management Board comprised of Bob as Managing Director, the Executive Director, a Company Secretary and then the five General Managers. Each of the companies acts as a stand-alone entity within a broad framework of Home Australia policies and standards.

Brand

Home Australia has five different brands that have developed in different ways. The Homestead brand has developed from a first home-buyer focus at the cheaper end of the market, to more of a quality mid-market placing, aimed at second home-buyers. Homestead has a strong community involvement and community focus.

Collier Homes in Western Australia and Huxley Homes in New South Wales are both 40-year-old brands that have a very good, solid, quality reputation in the middle of the market. New Start Homes in Queensland has always been an upmarket brand but is now trending downwards towards the volume segment of the market. Ashford in Victoria is a relatively new company and is positioning itself in the middle of the market.

Each of the brands uses the guiding principle and positioning statement of "Building Lasting Relationships". As Bob states, "For most of us, a home is much more than a place to live – it is a place to belong. Our homes reflect something of us – our tastes, our interests, our needs and our aspirations. Our homes also form a vital connection point in our lives for family, friends, and, thanks to technology, the wide world. In each of our homes resides our wish that you will build lasting relations with those people who are important to you. We try to achieve this by understanding that it is *your* home we are building, not ours".

Home Australia is remarkable because their focus is not just *what* people want but *why* they want it. To them, success in the housing industry and in home building is not about the house, it's about the relationships that people want with the company. Customers are out there looking for a good sales consultant to help them; it's not about producing the house, it's about marketing and distribution. This approach helps to account for Home Australia's success in the market place.

Strategic Issues

Home Australia faces a number of strategic issues including: a skills shortage; Government red tape; housing affordability; land shortages through planning regulation; and succession and exit strategies, which are of particular importance given Bob's impending move into federal politics.

INSIGHTS INTO

Building Your People to Build Your Business

Home Australia has been successful because of Bob Day's passion and commitment to sales, and the unique and outstanding process he calls "The Turtle on the Fence Post". What does that mean? Well, if you were ever to see a turtle sitting on top of a fence post, you would know that it didn't get there by itself – it had help to make it up that high. As a CEO, Bob knows that if he wants to achieve anything in business it has to be through people and he has applied his "turtle" concept to production, administration and, most importantly, sales.

The hardest and most important function in any business is sales. The difference between successful and unsuccessful companies is their ability to sell. Many companies pay lip service to sales but Home Australia has raised sales to the top of their agenda. They view sales as the "sharp end", "the exciting end", and "the flagship of the organisation".

"Staff in the sales department are the only ones who 'earn' the money. Everyone else 'spends' the money," says Bob. The competitive advantage of their organisation is sales and marketing. This is seen in their huge sales centre, surrounded by offices housing the team; in their rigorous selection process for sales consultants; in the induction and training process for sales consultants (using Home Australia's nationally tried and proven Sales Doctor® Training System); through the weekly inspirational sales meetings; the weekly and monthly rewards and awards; and their sales culture. Bob Day has systematically produced a sales culture that highly values and highly regards sales people. He has implemented an ongoing program that communicates to everyone in the organisation how highly the sales function is regarded. The Sales Doctor® Training System focuses on leadership, commitment to excellence, measurement, communication, strategy, vision, recruitment, continuous improvement and needs-based selling.

It is truly remarkable and refreshing to find an organisation that is so dedicated to being the best in the sales area. No wonder then that Home Australia has grown to be such a major national home-builder.

WHAT ARE THE SECRETS OF YOUR SUCCESS AS A CEO?

Lead by example. Ensure that you have an emotional connection with staff, practise honesty, wisdom and encouragement, be accessible, speak with authority about things, and give good advice and optimism.

What does successful CEO thinking take?

Competence and care. You've got to be competent; you've got to be really good; you've got to know your game; and you've got to be caring, with empathy.

What are the biggest challenges and opportunities of being a great CEO?

Challenges: To leave a lasting legacy.

Opportunities: To keep being a great leader, role model and example, and someone that all my staff and managers can be proud of.

What is the one thing, if it could be done, that would have the greatest impact on you as a CEO?

Having "10-out-of-10" managers. That would have the most impact on me – if the managers did what they know needs to be done.

What has been your biggest disappointment as a CEO?

The slowness of some states to perform adequately.

How do you handle rejection and failure?

I just look to the future, and know that I will solve this problem. Be persistent.

What key decisions have led to your success?

The expansions and acquisitions. I've put through the standard business model for all states with regular face-to-face benchmarking.

How many hours a week do you work?

I probably work about 60 hours.

How do you plan?

Daily to-do lists and then strategic lists with long-term goals. I do a little bit on the long-term ones on a regular basis and chip away at the big goals.

What are the major factors in your role as a CEO that have helped you, hindered you and blocked change?

Helped you: My personality, my nature, my optimism, my good health, and my ambition.

Hindered you: Poor management by GMs.

Blocked change: Poor management by GMs.

What part has innovation played in your company?

Not a big part, except for The Sales Doctor® program which is really innovative.

How and when have you transitioned your role?

I transitioned my role through appointing a General Manager to run each of the companies, and mentored each of them until they were able handle the role with minimal supervision.

What is your succession plan?

I am currently identifying a potential successor for the role of CEO of Home Australia.

What is your exit strategy?

To sell my shares through an Initial Public Offering (IPO).

What is business success to you?

A good brand, or a highly regarded brand in my industry and a successful IPO.

What problems do you, as a CEO, talk about on a day-to-day basis?

The state GMs' approach to dealing with issues and problems in their state, and the way they're handling it and managing it.

What are the issues that you have to deal with in your leadership role as a CEO?

Problems and crises in those various state divisions; I ask *them* how they're going to address it.

How has individual and group mentoring helped you?

By exposing me to different ideas, different people and different industries. I've seen that there are different types of people who have different approaches and different values in life. Some confirm that what I'm doing is right and some confirm that I'm different from them.

It's mattered enormously because everything stems from my level of wisdom, knowledge and understanding of the world – how it works and the people in it, what motivates people and how to manage people, how to change policies in fields and how to be a leader in my industry. Having a mentor for almost 20 years has had a tremendous impact on helping me clarify these things.

What changes have you observed in the workplace culture to remain competitive to employ Generation Y?

There's no veneration of the CEO. People in authority are not viewed the same as (they used to be). The attitude towards authority and the boss is completely different. I have juniors who have no qualms about walking in and saying, "Bob, I was thinking such and such".

What impact has the business had on your life?

It's a great adventure, and there is this quote of Shakespeare's, "There is a tide in the affairs of men, which, taken at the flood, leads on to fortune. Omitted, all the voyage of their life is bound in shallows and in miseries". In other words, to enjoy success, you have to take opportunity when and where it comes.

What have you learned about yourself?

That I am self-doubting and insecure, but ambitious. That regardless of limitations and weaknesses, I can accomplish anything.

What have you learned about people?

That they do things for their reasons, not yours.

What impact has the business had on your life?

It's exposed me to the world's best ideas, to some of the brightest people and the most interesting people, and it has given me a platform to fulfil all my dreams and ambitions.

Do you have to sacrifice your own life and family to be successful in business? Any comments?

Well, it's a matter of degrees. Yes, we all sacrifice to some degree our family, our lives, our personal interests, but the challenge is to get the right balance of how much we forego seeing our children and our spouse. At what point is it too much? I'm active in public policy areas and community activities. I do a lot of promotion for, and write a lot of papers, articles and letters about, home ownership, housing affordability and youth employment matters. I was not born into wealth or privilege. My parents were working class and we lived in a house built by the Housing Trust. But so what? As the old saying goes, "Each of us must accept the cards life deals us. But once they are in our hands, we alone get to decide how to play those cards in order to win the game".

How have you capitalised on your business and developed it in an extraordinary way, geometrically?

By using my business as a platform into community and public policy areas here and overseas – for example, being involved with the Housing the Homeless Council, Work for the Dole National Committee and the Great Australian Dream project, which provide global exposure for, and international involvement with, housing affordability.

How has your development as a leader maximised your impact on all of the stakeholders you work with?

With energy and ideas.

How has your life developed to make you a better person and how have you maximised this?

By treating everyone I meet with respect, and accepting that everybody I meet knows something that I don't. Even the guy who washes my car every Friday knows things I don't.

Lessons you have Learned as a CEO

The future belongs not to those who know how to make things, but to those who know how to sell things. In other words, success in business is no longer about production; it's about marketing and distribution.

Whoever sets the price; the other sets the terms. When negotiating, I don't mind whether the other person sets the price of the deal or the terms. If they want to set the price, I set the terms. If they want to set the terms, then I'll set the price, but they can take their pick. Let the other party choose first.

People do things for their reasons, not yours.

Job descriptions are absolutely useless. People will always end up doing what they like doing, no matter what's on the job description.

We all must suffer one type of pain – either the pain of discipline or the pain of regret. But we get to choose which one. The pain of discipline is measured in grams; the pain of regret is measured in tonnes. One must suffer one kind of pain or the other, take your pick.

Calm seas don't make good sailors. You've got to go through the wilderness to get to the Promised Land.

Remember the importance of the little things – punctuality, tidiness, courtesy, politeness, respect.

No matter how up-lifting or significant education or exposure to high ideals and ideas might be, it all leaves you magnificently unprepared for the long littleness of life. In other words, 99% of life as a CEO is long, long littleness; only 1% is the big strategic stuff.

Never give up – have persistence.

The importance of being inherently dissatisfied with the status quo.

The more authority you get, the less the power. In other words, the higher up the ladder you go, the less power you have.

Final Word

Be charitable. Give and keep giving, and practise until you get really good at giving of yourself, your time, your money, your thoughts, and your resources.

Questions for Contemplation

As you reflect on Bob's life, ask yourself:

1. How could I do more to give and encourage others to give?

2. Everyone has goals they want to achieve, problems they want to solve and fears they want to overcome. How could I be more effective in encouraging other people to tackle their problems in order to achieve their destiny?

3. Do you know what your destiny is? If not, how will you discover this?

4. Do you know how you're going in achieving your goals, solving your problems and overcoming your fears? If not, what do you need to do to learn these skills?

Favorite Book

The Purpose Driven Life, by Rick Warren

Contact Details

Bob Day

CEO, Home Australia Pty Ltd

Email: bobday@homeaustralia.com.au

Websites: www.homeaustralia.com.au | www.nationbuild.com

www.makin.com.au | www.greataustraliandream.net.au

Developing a Culture of Innovation and Risk Taking

How would you transform and double a law firm in just four years in a competitive environment?

Nigel McBride

Born: 1955

Education: Bachelor of Laws (LLB), Canterbury University, New Zealand, 1980. Post-graduate qualifications for admissions in the Supreme Courts of New Zealand, South Australia, Western Australia and the High Court of Australia.

Career: Management, sales, marketing and legal roles in the pharmaceutical, financial and trustee industries, New Zealand, 1980-90; Senior Legal Consultant, Health Department of Western Australia, 1990-93; Director of Legal Administration, Health Department of Western Australia, 1993-95; Senior Legal Consultant, Minter Ellison, Perth, 1995-98; Director of Professional Services (COO role), Minter Ellison, Perth, 1998-2000; Chief Executive Partner, Minter Ellison, Adelaide, 2000-present;

Personal: Nigel is married with two children. He likes to travel, to write, record and perform music, to read and write books, enjoys the performing arts, and food and wine.

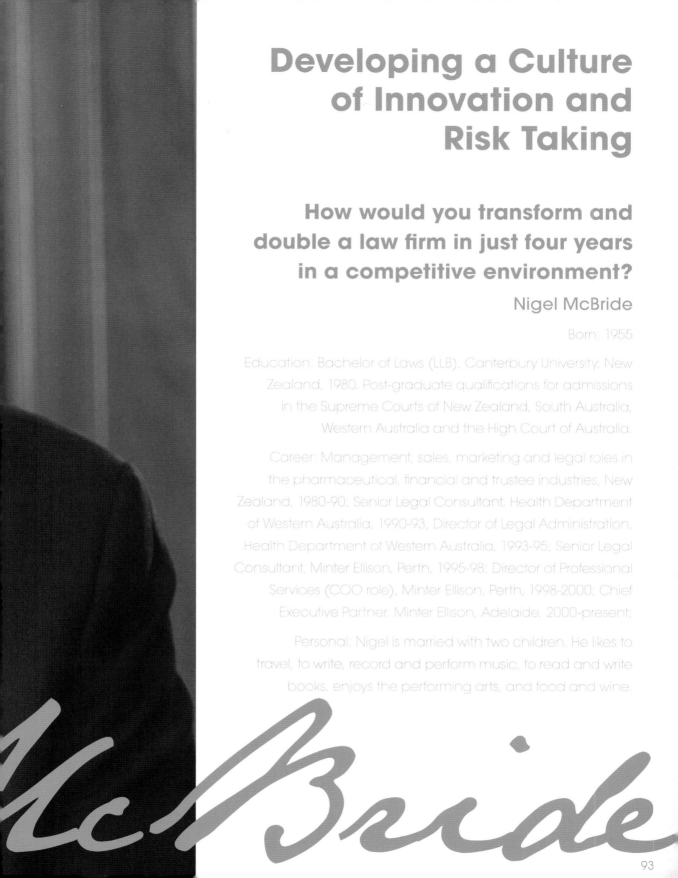

"Instead of conforming to what you believe you should be, be who you are, be passionate about who you are, be authentic. It doesn't matter if you're an introvert or an extrovert, it doesn't matter if you're good at physics or you're good at sales; what people are looking for today is authenticity."

Company Profile

In the last five years, Minter Ellison South Australia has experienced compound double-digit top-line growth to become South Australia's largest law firm with a dominant market share estimated to exceed 30% of the South Australian legal services market. In 2003, Minter Ellison opened a Northern Territory office which has since tripled in size. The company is a stand-alone partnership and is not financially integrated with the Minter Ellison east coast firm.

The firm has achieved an outstanding profile, brand and reputation reflected, for example, with back-to-back BRW/St George awards for the Best Professional Services Firm in South Australia for 2005 and 2006. It is recognised as a firm with great clients, great people and great infrastructure. It is an excellent example of innovation and diversity in areas such as using leading technology-leveraged solutions to provide a new paradigm in cost and services such as WorkCover disputes (where the firm replaced a panel of eight other firms to become the sole legal provider), credit management, claims management and franchising. The firm has practiced prudent overhead control even with its new building fit-out and impending relocation. Since 1997/98 it has grown its revenue from $10.5 million to over $36 million and is arguably the only firm with the kind of local breadth and depth in the state to be correctly regarded as a "full service" commercial law firm.

Products and Services

Minter Ellison is a full-service commercial legal firm.

Growth Trends

Minter Ellison's strategy for growth and success occurred in two broad steps under Nigel's leadership. The first step took place from 2001 to 2004 and entailed an aggressive pursuit of market leaders and benchmarks to drive quality and profitability. Inevitably, this meant changing nearly 50% of the partners and staff. As well as retaining the firm's best, Nigel led an aggressive lateral recruitment strategy to target not only the best people in the South Australian market but also to attract top professionals from the east coast and overseas. This single strategy of "moving to quality" across every aspect of the firm, including management and support staff, was the biggest factor driving growth and success during this period. These changes significantly increased the firm's profile and dramatically improved their ability to take business from competitors and attract "top shelf" work from both within and outside South Australia.

The second step was to embrace innovation and technology as fundamental business drivers. This meant becoming technologically savvy across every area of the business including communications, document production, case flow and electronic file management, and extranets.

During this period the South Australian legal industry experienced enormous upheaval, with many practices reducing significantly in size and/or moving towards an east coast focus by opening offices in places like Sydney and Melbourne. Minter Ellison remains the only South Australian-focused major firm in Adelaide.

Performance

A major investment in time, resources and personnel went into technology-driven "volume" markets where transaction costs could be reduced significantly because of lower Adelaide overheads as well other services with a nexus to legal services and statutory compliance. These areas included claims management; leasing and licensing management; transaction-based insurance; secured and unsecured recoveries; conveyancing; and franchising.

Structure

From 2000 to 2005, the structure became flatter and more corporatised, with equity partners having less and less direct involvement in the day-to-day running of the business. This is now handled by Nigel as the Chief Executive Partner (CEP); he is assisted by a Chief Operating Officer and a Chief Financial Officer. There are six partners who coordinate the practice areas. The CEP sits on the Board, and reports to a Chairman and five representative partners elected by the equity partnership, plus one external director. The Board reports to a quarterly meeting of the partners.

Brand

The Minter Ellison brand was developed through a focus on becoming the best law firm in Adelaide, with the best people in every area of practice. A second strategy in brand development was to offer clients technology-leveraged solutions for legal services at a fixed price. A third strategy was to get into new markets such as claims management and credit management. A further strategy was to become a national centre for innovative business solutions based in Adelaide.

The open, transparent, vibrant and accessible culture

that Nigel has fostered has been particularly attractive to Generation Y lawyers. Nigel has always led from the front and in his early days would go to the "opening of an envelope" to ensure that the firm was being represented out in the market. He became a micro-brand of the firm and is now intentionally beginning a strategy to hand that on to the partners, many of whom have now become significant leaders in their own industry and practice areas.

Strategic Issues

Minter Ellison needs to focus on: the South Australian market size; growth; lack of large corporates; pricing; lack of investment; and a conservative state government in terms of spending on legal outsourcing. Other strategic issues include: growing an already dominant market share; the Darwin market, quality, parochialism, market size, isolation and profitability; salary and overhead growth creating margin squeeze as top-line growth slows; access to east coast markets; and maintaining the investment in specialists.

INSIGHTS INTO

Law firms have never been at the cutting edge of change and innovation. How do you take an inherently conservative culture and lead a group of lawyers into embracing the kind of innovation and risk taking that has attracted client accolades and national recognition?

Nigel would offer that the answer is enthusiastic and challenging leadership that encourages and rewards innovation. People are attracted to his strong vision, which he shares passionately and with authenticity. Nigel has continuously reinvented his enthusiasm and has focused strongly on excellence, which to him is non-negotiable. He has creatively enabled the firm to achieve thought leadership in a number of areas and is able to relate to and inspire his staff. His focus now is on developing a people-based, sustainable culture where everything gets constructively challenged and where people are empowered.

Accompanying this is Nigel's clarity in setting a "stretch" strategic direction aimed at continuing to dominate the local market rather than taking the standard option of opening offices on the east coast of Australia. To stay strongly based in Adelaide has been a risk in itself – but the risk has certainly been worth taking for Minter Ellison.

Operating as a CEO

WHAT ARE THE SECRETS OF YOUR SUCCESS AS A CEO?

> I love people. You cannot lead a people organisation unless you have a genuine empathy for people, because they know when you really care and when you don't.

I absolutely believe that culture is not negotiable. If you have a winning culture, that's very, very hard to beat. I also believe that humour is incredibly important. We take what we do seriously, but, for goodness sake, let's not take ourselves *too* seriously.

What does successful CEO thinking take?

You've got to constantly ask yourself, "Where are my blind spots?" You've got to be open to and challenged by your trusted senior managers and your partner colleagues. You also have to continually challenge them.

And I like to soak up ideas; I want to find out what has made other people successful. One thing that TEC (a CEO mentoring group) has really brought home to me is that in every industry the strategic and business issues are all basically the same.

What are the biggest challenges and opportunities of being a great CEO?

Challenges: I started off with an incredibly ambitious, almost science-fiction-like(!!), five-year strategic plan and I've exceeded every stretch goal I had back then. The challenge is how you keep reinventing the passion for the organisation and not to accept the apparent market and opportunity boundaries that others do.

Adelaide is an inherently conservative town with a thin regional economy that could not support a law firm that's very much bigger than ours. For us, to have the growth we've had is extraordinary under these circumstances. So, I think the size of the market and where it's heading is a challenge. Another thing is, how on earth do you maintain compound double-digit top-line growth year after year!?

Opportunities: Opportunities are definitely there to take one of the best, newly reinvigorated firms in the Australian legal scene and go into new markets, be cutting-edge in technology solutions, and really be innovative in things like partnering with clients.

What is the one thing, if it could be done, that would have the greatest impact on you as a CEO?

It would be if I got one day a week or a fortnight where I wasn't contactable and all I did was vision-casting about the business and looking for the next great opportunity – really stepping away from the business to work on it instead of in it all the time. Unfortunately I still "drown" in too much detail and this is in spite of having a great Board and a top management team.

What has been your biggest disappointment as a CEO?

No matter how innovative we are, how many awards we get, or how much we grow (and we've had extraordinary growth), there is still a "cringe" in much of Sydney or Melbourne about recognising the value and quality of Adelaide lawyers.

How do you handle rejection and failure?

Rejection can be pretty tough, because while I come across as being a hard, driven kind of guy, the truth is that I'm pretty soft underneath. I don't handle rejection and failure as well as I could.

I think that, as a leader and CEO, I've been really successful in the last few years, but I haven't always been. I think failure is a great reality check and an opportunity to stop being a "legend in your own lunchtime". It's not just all about me. I've found that I've learned more in failure than I have in success.

What key decisions have led to your success?

I put my career and job on the line to turn the firm around, and, especially in the early days, that meant on a number of occasions that it was either me or somebody else who was going to go. You've got to have an enormous amount of personal courage to take on a major change management role.

How many hours a week do you work?

50-60 hours.

How do you plan?

Electronic diary management is really important. I block out free time or time for strategic issues and make sure my Personal Assistant is very careful about the appointments she puts in. I personally check my time and commitments on a weekly, monthly and quarterly basis.

We have 3-5 year strategic directions, an annual business plan, quarterly budgets and plans, and business development plans that are measured monthly, quarterly and annually.

What are the major factors in your role as a CEO that have helped you, hindered you and blocked change?

Helped you: The absolute imperative I received was to improve the business from of the state the firm was in when I arrived. The trust and support of my Chairman, our Board, my partners and my management team has been absolutely pivotal and I regard myself as privileged to be in a firm that is as cohesive as ours.

Hindered you: Inherent conservatism of this market and of law firms generally. Getting the right people remains the single biggest key and the biggest potential hurdle to our continued growth.

Blocked change: The time it takes to do something, to push it through, because you can't simply impose change no matter how obvious or logical it seems to you.

What part has innovation played in your company?

Massive. One of the things we'd say about our culture is that it is an incubator for innovation. Our culture creates an environment where innovation is recognised, rewarded and celebrated.

How and when have you transitioned your role?

I think I've transitioned it from an externally recruited "head kicker" who came in to do some fundamental change management in a necessarily short time to an effective leader of a successful, high-growth firm at the top of our market.

What is your succession plan?

I'm about to commit to a final five years as Chief Executive Partner. Towards the end of that time I will bring through a successor.

What is your exit strategy?

Working in a consulting role to the firm after I go, which will be part of settling down my successor and ensuring momentum for business development between us. I'll still remain an ambassador for the firm.

What is business success to you?

It's creating a sustainable winning culture that attracts and retains top talent. Top people attract great clients who bring interesting and profitable work, which in turn leads to attracting great people, and so on. It's a winning self-fulfilling cycle that can have an unstoppable momentum if it's led properly.

What problems do you, as a CEO, talk about on a day-to-day basis?

Time management for the senior management team. How to beat the silo culture (we're now on multiple sites) and how to keep cohesion in a rapidly growing law firm. Getting the balance right between being market focused and internally focused. Spending time building the business in a macro sense, but having the personal time to sit down with the key internal stakeholders, like my partners and senior managers. We are all time poor, so the urgent always seems to overcome the important.

What are the issues that you have to deal with in your leadership role as a CEO?

Business discipline – there is no substitute for this. Focus – it's so easy to waste time on stuff that doesn't count. I also have to be the enforcer of our culture and values. We have a saying: "values are not about having some statement on the wall, it's about holding people accountable for their behaviors and attitudes."

How do you allow the space and time for creative thinking for yourself and your staff?

There's not enough. I get creative time in the car driving home, on an aircraft, in an airport lounge. I think creativity comes to you at all times of the night and day and I think you've just got to be tuned in for it. At least once a week my key managers and I do some brainstorming.

How has individual and group mentoring helped you?

It has been essential. It's important because it helps you access your values and priorities; it helps you take a reality check and it helps you to see your blind spots.

What changes have you observed in the workplace culture to remain competitive to employ Generation Y?

Our culture is very amenable to the collegial approach that Generation Y thrives on; the recognition and value; doing exciting, fun work; being rewarded; working in a non-hierarchical and transparent environment.

What impact has the business had on your life?

It's given me the opportunity to prove to myself that I've got the drive and ability to achieve significant tasks that I put my mind to.

Do you have to sacrifice your own life and family to be successful in business? Any comments?

Theoretically, no, you shouldn't have to. Have I discovered how to do that? No. My point is I think I've paid a relatively high price in the last six years with my family and time to get this business to where it is. I don't think you can be genuinely successful in business or in life unless you get that balance right. Many CEOs have had their marriages disintegrate, their health suffer badly; or they're just fundamentally unhappy – you can't honestly describe that as success. Ensure that you look after yourself and your personal relationships and do the things that you truly want to do with your own life. Then look after the needs of the business.

How have you capitalised on your business and developed it in an extraordinary way, geometrically?

We've leveraged it. We've taken one piece of technology and rolled it out, for example, across 25 different business and practice areas. We've used that knowledge across a number of areas. We've leveraged the same methodology across a large number of other clients.

How has your development as a leader maximised your impact on all of the stakeholders you work with?

I've learned to actively listen more. My definition of boring used to be when other people were talking when I should have been! Delegating, even though people won't do it the way I would. That was a huge one, because I was such a control freak. Now, the more I stand back and empower them, the better we're going to be. I've got to make myself replaceable in those areas that dilute the real impact I can have as a strategic leader.

How has your life developed to make you a better person and how have you maximised this?

I think I came into Adelaide and this firm with something to prove. I've relaxed a lot, so I think that's made me a better person. I've got my sense of humour back. I'd like to think that I've developed a lot more empathy, so when I make hard decisions (and I've had to make a large number of them) I now have a greater sense of connection even in the tough times. You never want to get to the point where a hard decision becomes easy.

Lessons you have Learned as a CEO

People are everything.

Leadership means personal cost. Be prepared to pay it otherwise don't put yourself in a leadership position.

The essential ingredient in leadership is the ability to relate to, inspire and motivate people. People skills are not an option for a leader; you've got to have them, and if you don't have them, you've got to develop them.

EVERYBODY finds change threatening, but constant change in response to your business environment, culture and so on is not optional, it is essential.

People are attracted to strong vision and strong visionaries. People want to be led, they want to be inspired, they want to be excited, they want to feel like they're part of a team that's going somewhere – and that's infectious. It creates an environment that's wonderful to work in.

Clients aren't an interruption to your business; they ARE your business. Your competitors can always deliver what you can; it comes down to how you deliver it and how you connect with your clients.

Never create a strategy that's going to be easily achieved; it's got to be a stretch and you've got to constantly review it.

Have the discipline to reinvest in your people, innovation, and research and development. Resist the temptation to pull all of the cash out of the business. You're there to ensure investment happens for the long haul.

Learn to celebrate success and make recognising people in your organisation one of your great themes.

Understand that sometimes you have to make hard business decisions, but there's a way of carrying

Nigel McBride

them out that is morally and ethically correct.

Integrity always pays in the long-term. Do the right thing, even if it costs you more in the first instance.

Stop having a messianic complex. You are not the Messiah; you can't solve everything.

Don't live in regret; move on.

Have the courage to commit to what you said you'd do – push through.

Have the courage to demand accountability from your colleagues.

Have an absolute commitment to a people-based culture that you are proud of.

Excellence is non-negotiable. That must always be the benchmark. Anybody can be mediocre.

Final Word

I'd like to reproduce leaders with a contagious ability to impart vision.

Questions for Contemplation

Reflecting on the life and experiences that Nigel has had, ask yourself:

1. If, in such a relatively short time, Nigel could create a cutting-edge innovation culture in one of the world's most conservative professions (and in an ultra-conservative city), what is stopping you from delivering that in your life and business?

2. How do you make running your business fun for your people? How do you celebrate success and recognise people in a way that becomes a hallmark of your business?

3. How inspiring and creative are you?

4. Do you attract people just by virtue of the fact that you've got passion about what you're doing and a great sense of self-belief? What impact do you have on people?

Favorite Book

Funky Business: Talent Makes Capital Dance, by Jonas Ridderstråle and Kjell Nordström

Contact Details

Nigel McBride, Chief Executive Partner

Minter Ellison Lawyers SA/NT

Email: nigel.mcbride@minterellison.com

Website: www.minterellison.com

Mike

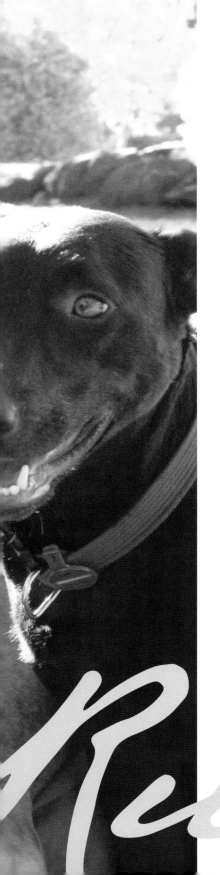

Managing Not for Profit Organisations

How would you run a not for profit organisation while preserving its values?

Mike Rungie

Born: 1946

Education: B. Science (Hons), PhD, University of Adelaide, 1972; Visiting scholar, University of Syracuse, 1987; Member, The Executive Connection, 1998-present.

Career: Marketing Manager, Women's Division of Clark's Shoes, Melbourne, 1972-75; Manager of Services, Spastic Society of Victoria, 1975-79; Manager of Services, ACH Group, 1980-96; CEO, ACH Group, 1997-present.

Personal: Mike enjoys skiing, bush-walking, swimming, time with his family, community activities, cards, music, films, theatre, travel and tinkering.

"Not-for-profits have a clearly defined purpose which is not about profit and consumption. That suits me really well. This organisation is about growing communities, about older people being productive, about relationships staying in place, about people growing and learning".

Background

ACH Group is a not-for-profit public benevolent institution providing aged care mostly in South Australia. It changed its name from "aged cottage homes" to "aged care and housing" and ultimately became ACH Group when it appreciated that older people preferred support in living a good life to the somewhat demoralising aged care alternative.

The organisation has grown significantly over the years and in 2005/2006 had revenue of $54 million and an operating surplus of $0.5 million. ACH Group has 1,300 staff and 900 volunteers. It operates seven nursing homes supporting 1,200 people per year. It provides 800 in-home care packages supporting 1,200 people per year. Other community services support 32,000 people per year. ACH Group also manages 660 houses accommodating 700 people.

Mike Rungie was appointed CEO in 1997 after serving in Executive Management roles for 16 years. He has a passion for aged care and enjoys running a not-for-profit organisation because of its pre-eminent focus on values and community.

Products and Services

ACH Group provides services to older people including housing, home support, hostel and nursing home services, an extensive range of short-term respite, convalescent and rehabilitation services, and some services to improve people's health and well being.

Growth Trends

The growth of ACH Group is related to its core purpose of facilitating communities of productive, growing, learning, older people who have the opportunity to maintain and develop positive relationships and roles. The vision, mission and values of this organisation relate to older people as active, valued and contributing members of family, community and society. The vision is achieved by supporting and valuing staff, family and volunteers who work together to provide services for these older people.

According to its 2005-2010 Strategic Plan, the organisation's intention is to almost double the number of clients it supports from 25,000 to 45,000. The growth focus will track consumer preference, encourage people to improve in situations of difficult health, encourage positive ageing, and focus on supporting people at home.

ACH Group's most significant change in the last three years has been the provision of short-term packages of care. These have reduced the need for hospital admission as well as providing rehabilitation and high quality level of care following discharge from hospitals. Growth has mostly been achieved through winning tenders, inventing new work and convincing the Government to joint venture with ACH Group outside of the tender process. There have also been some mergers and acquisitions, joint ventures and alliances.

Performance

ACH Group has performed well over the last five years, growing from revenue of $31 million in 2001/2002, to revenue of $54 million and surplus of $0.5 million in 2005/2006. It has achieved a high level of quality accreditation and positioned itself well with other people and organisations.

Mike Rungie is committed and passionate about doing something useful for older people and Australia. He could have grown the organisation more quickly by doing "more of the same", as some competitors have done. Instead, he chose to focus on innovation.

There are 3 main products in aged care: aged care facilities (nursing homes and hostels), community care packages, and retirement housing. These are operated by both not-for-profits and the commercial sector. Quality of the products is already high and industry focus is on more of the same.

There is a growing preference from consumers for home care and continuation of their "good lives". They don't view aged care with optimism and are particularly clear that they don't want to live in a nursing home. There is also government concern about rising health and aged care costs, with governments starting to look for prevention, efficiencies and user-pays systems.

ACH Group's focus on customers, service, innovation, partnerships and capital raising has positioned it well to be a leader in this sector in the next five years.

Structure

ACH Group is a public benevolent institution. Its assets are owned by the members who are all on the Board. If the organisation stops trading, the assets are passed on to an organisation with similar values and goals. There are currently 11 Board members with provision for 12. Members are appointed for up to three terms of three years through a skills audit of the existing Board and needs identified by the strategic plan.

The CEO has a team of five senior executives: a General Manager Corporate Services; a General Manager Property and Housing; a General Manager Community Services; a General Manager Residential Services; and a General Manager Business Development. There is also a Manager for Research and Development who assists the CEO.

Brand

Historically, ACH Group hasn't needed a strong brand. The organisation has always experienced high demand for services, received sufficient funds and had an abundance of staff without strong brand recognition. Now, however, there is strong competition for staff, funding, volunteers and partners. Suddenly it has become very important for ACH Group to have a strong brand and brand message to enable it to stand out from competitors. A re-branding exercise is needed to build on the unique fundamentals of ACH Group – service when you need it, not products you fit into, and positive ageing, not aged care.

Strategic Issues

The most important strategic issues facing ACH Group include: attraction and retention of staff; ongoing development of the culture; positive ageing; ease of access to services; sustainability; forming strong alliances; growth through acquisitions, mergers and joint ventures; strengthening the ACH brand; and open community governance.

Managing Not-for-Profit Organisations

Success hinges on the organisation's purpose and the people it attracts at all levels. The purpose of ACH Group is developing communities of productive, learning, growing, older people in meaningful relationships and roles. It is significantly different from an organisation focused on profit. The alignment of people at all levels with the values of the organisation is critical. It is clear that commitment is alive at ACH Group. The culture, people and processes all reflect the prevailing philosophy of service, support and care. ACH Group believes that people aren't that interested in making money for the boss and capitalises on attracting people to ACH Group with the primary goal of caring. ACH Group's challenge is to then unite the team around growing this nurturing to ensure clients have less dependency and a full life. This aim really attracts staff, but is tough to do on a daily basis. ACH Group has developed its own "customer impact statements" which engage staff in the dilemma that while quality of care is usually high, quality of life can be quite low.

It helps to have a visionary leader who is passionately committed to positive ageing. Mike is not content simply to emulate the "business" success becoming so dominant in aged care. Rather, he is committed to developing a more relevant, more client-focused, more holistic and flexible approach to meeting the needs of older people. He has clearly focused on this and has built an excellent team to support this vision. The development of the whole leadership team is another reason for this organisation's outstanding success. ACH Group is run to make an annual surplus that is used to fund R&D and growth. Growth is a goal only where it achieves good quality support to older people, innovation and (usually) economies of scale.

WHAT ARE THE SECRETS OF YOUR SUCCESS AS A CEO?

I'm not a generic CEO. I believe in this business. It interests and excites me. I think of it as a marathon, staying in front for many years. I need clarity of direction and measurable goals, structuring the right jobs for the time and then placing the right people in them, and constant learning through the mentoring process. I work at staying healthy and fit, at being loving, eating well, sleeping well and having a different life outside work.

What does successful CEO thinking take?

You need to live in the space of where the organisation is going – not where it is.

What are the biggest challenges and opportunities of being a great CEO?

Challenges: As tempting as it may be, the challenge is to avoid flogging dead horses, old ideas and methods, products that people don't want, and staff who do not want to be there.

Opportunities: There is a once-in-a-lifetime chance to harness a lot of resources to create something for clients, staff and citizens.

What is the one thing, if it could be done, that would have the greatest impact on you as a CEO?

I would turn the clock back 10 years, but take all my present knowledge and experience with me. If I had known then what I know now, I would have invested so much more in building the skills and strengths of the people around me, and would then have been able to create so much more.

What has been your biggest disappointment as a CEO?

I wasted time. I could have got going quicker. I could have driven the team better and developed people around me better.

What key decisions led to your success?

I don't have an image of being successful; I didn't even want to be a CEO. So letting friends and mentors push me out of my comfort zone when making (or avoiding) decisions has been critical.

How many hours a week do you work?

It varies. 50 would be typical and it's sometimes 60.

How do you plan?

Formally and informally – the creative parts never seem to happen formally. With others and alone. At work and away from work. All the time – not once a year for two days.

What are the major factors in your role as a CEO that have helped you, hindered you and blocked change?

Helped you: The Executive team kicking the ball in the same direction and to one another – having them get creative about issues that matter and not giving up; seeing them move into one another's patches as the work demands change; watching them lift their performance as the bar rises; having them develop CEO mindsets about their own divisions; and having them behave like a Board in that they view the organisation as a whole, and not just as separate divisions.

Hindered you: Not focusing on the above.

Blocked change: My own lack of willingness to address issues.

What part has innovation played in your company?

Innovation has delivered us new services, new funding and a culture that people are attracted to.

How and when have you transitioned your role?

From operational to strategic, from being an "answers man" to being a coach, from ACH Group working alone to ACH Group joint-venturing.

What is your succession plan?

That the top 20 staff are all very strong. That the Board is so engaged in our unique competitive advantage that they can easily spot the next (and most suitable) CEO. That we have set up opportunities and alliances for the long-term future.

What is your exit strategy?

I don't have one.

What is business success to you?

That we survived; that people look to ACH Group as a community partner in creating ageing that is positive; that the business is full of good people who add value to the team effort; that people enjoyed themselves, made some money along the way and never got bored.

What problems do you, as a CEO, talk about on a day-to-day basis?

Engaging staff, raising quality, better use of finances, paying attention to our alliances and government and managing risk.

What are the issues that you have to deal with in your leadership role as a CEO?

Creating possibilities in others and then aligning these into a team effort.

How has individual and group mentoring helped you?

I don't think I would be here without it. I've learned beyond my own patch and years. TEC (a CEO mentoring organisation) demands you be a great student and a great teacher.

What changes have you observed in the workplace culture to remain competitive to employing Generation Y?

People might think that aged care wouldn't attract young people but young people love it. It's probably because there is a lot of autonomy at all levels. There's a tonne of room for professional expression, innovation, sincerity and career development. We are creating ourselves as a training workplace for undergraduates and graduates, and that's increasing our numbers of younger people. Ultimately, if our care is enabling good lives for older people, then they will join us. If it's compassionate but gloomy care they won't.

What impact has the business had on your life?

If being productive (without causing too much

harm) is the ultimate, then this business gets close to the ultimate. My job is what lots of people do for fun as a volunteer, when they are not at work!

Do you have to sacrifice your own life and family to be successful in business? Any comments?

Yes and no – my family like me better when I am inspired and hate me when I'm bored, so if I'm sometimes absent (or present and overbearing) they probably wouldn't have it any other way. You wouldn't want to miss the incredible upside of a job like this. Don't start telling yourself you are making sacrifices.

How have you capitalised on your business and developed it in an extraordinary way, geometrically?

The extraordinary development hasn't been growth, it's been focusing on "life" not "care". Would you want two weeks respite in a nursing home or two weeks on holiday at the beach with a couple of fun-loving volunteers? The problem is, even in not-for-profits, the trophies are for growth not purpose.

How has your development as a leader maximised your impact on all of the stakeholders you work with?

I aim to know who all the stakeholders are and to be consistent with the ACH Group story that I am telling. We work in layers with stakeholders so that Board and Executive leadership are doing the same thing at different levels.

How has your life developed to make you a better person and how have you maximised this?

As my skills and confidence have increased, so has my trust in others. The fear is slowly going. I used to appoint people I could delegate to; now I appoint people I can trust.

Lessons you have Learned as a CEO

Behave like you are five years out.

Be like a coach of a high performance team.

Hire slow, fire fast.

Create the vision with your team, tell them the story and make the brand the story.

Exploit your strengths and build others into your weak areas.

Never compromise your efforts to stay fresh and healthy.

Love your clients.

Always move forward, even when you are retreating.

Watch the bottom line like a pervert.

Get out more – out of your square, out of your company and out of your country.

Become a CEO, not a COO (Chief Operating Officer).

Find some mentors (they won't find you).

Genuinely understand the suffering in old age.

Most strategic planning is only continuous improvement.

Getting the right people on the executive team is one of the most important things you can do. But if you don't keep shaping and growing that team to match the growth of the organisation, you will have to keep changing the team's membership.

Pay attention to health and holidays.

Seek personal financial advice. It gives you autonomy in the way you deal with the business.

Do lots of learning outside the business.

Mike Rungie

Final Word

Growth and development is better than standing still. I see it in the lives of the people around me, in my staff, in my family and in older people. A life without growth and development is like death.

Questions for Contemplation

As you reflect on Mike's life, ask yourself:

1. What questions are you currently contemplating about your life?

2. If you are in transition, how do you grow forward while actually handing over and letting go?

3. The purpose of Mike's not-for-profit organisation is about growing communities, about older people being productive, about relationships staying in place and about people growing and learning. It is not about making goods for consumption and profit. What could you take from not-for-profits and apply to for-profit organisations?

4. When you are growing an organisation rapidly, how can you build a successful executive team?

Favorite Books

Passing Program Analysis of Service Systems Implementation of Normalization Goals, by Wolf Wolfensberger

Good to Great, by Jim Collins

Contact Details

Dr Mike Rungie, CEO

ACH Group

E-mail: mrungie@ach.org.au

Website: www.ach.org.au

Leading and Managing an Infrastructure Company

How would you run a company with government constraints, fixed income and limited flexibility?

Ian Stirling

Born: 1950

Education: Matriculation, Marcellin College Melbourne; B. Business (Accounting/Law), Swinburne Institute of Technology; Certified Practising Accountant (CPA); Advanced Management and Leadership Courses, Melbourne University and Templeton College, Oxford University.

Career: Project Director, Corporatisation Taskforce, State Electricity Commission (VIC); Manager, Strategic Change, National Electricity (VIC); Chief Financial Officer, PowerNet (VIC); Chief Financial Officer, GPU PowerNet (VIC); Chief Financial Officer (1999-2001), General Manager Revenue Reset (2001-02) and CEO (2002-present) of ElectraNet (SA).

Personal: Married with three children. Interests include baroque and ancient music, history, reading and most sports.

Overview of ElectraNet

"It's not your right to challenge; it's your responsibility. The reality is you can go through 20 different pathways to reach a conclusion. If you're not challenged you'll revert to your favourite way and it may limit you from getting the best outcome."

Background

ElectraNet is a highly regulated company. Essentially a monopoly, it has to present a plan to a regulating body every five years seeking approval for its prices. ElectraNet came out of the former ETSA Corporation, which was corporatised in 1997. At this stage, ETSA was broken up into a number of companies responsible for generating power; one transmission company (ElectraNet), one distribution company (ETSA Utilities) and one retail company (ETSA Power). All these businesses were later privatised in one guise or another.

ElectraNet is a single-purpose electricity transmission infrastructure company. Over 90% of its business is regulated via a known revenue stream, which will continue until 2008. It is a privately owned company with four shareholders and was privatised in 2000. Its current assets are sound and are presently valued at $1.4 billion.

The company has had a major challenge changing the culture from a quasi-public enterprise to a commercial operation. In 2003 ElectraNet was downsized by 25%. This provided the opportunity to implement a new culture dubbed the "ElectraNet Way".

ElectraNet was and is required to invest around $370 million into new regulated capital projects during the period July 2003 – June 2008. This is nearly 300% more than in the previous five-year period. It also invested about $80 million in unregulated infrastructure. It is currently planning an application for a revenue cap for the following five-year period with an expectation that over $700 million will need to be invested. ElectraNet is a high performing company with a highly competent workforce. It operates under constant scrutiny to maintain a continuous supply of electricity.

Products and Services

ElectraNet owns, operates and manages the electricity transmission network throughout South Australia. It specialises in the transmission of electricity at high voltage over long distances and to remote areas. There are three major sources of power generation in South Australia: power stations at Port Augusta, Torrens Island and Pelican Point. Generators of electricity using brown coal, distillate oil, natural gas and wind, use ElectraNet's transmission network to transport their electricity. ElectraNet's network extends over 200,000 square kilometers via 6,000 circuit kilometres of lines and 76 substations. There is also an interconnection to the national electricity market via two regulated interconnections in Victoria. ElectraNet delivers 99% of ETSA Utilities' power – the distributor for SA. ETSA Utilities then distributes it down South Australian streets where it is sold by three principal retailers – AGL, Origin and TRUenergy. ElectraNet also directly connects other major users of power in South Australia including BHPB and Santos.

Growth Trends

The company has grown in accordance with its strategic plan from $150 million revenue and 115 employees in 2003, to projected 2008 figures of $200 million revenue and 200 employees. ElectraNet operates under a five-

Ian Stirling

year plan for revenue and capital, approved by a national regulator. Growth is controlled by this plan in line with market development. Around 10% of ElectraNet's sales come from the unregulated transmission market. There are major opportunities for ElectraNet to grow sales in the unregulated market in areas such as the Roxby Downs expansion and other resource developments throughout the state.

Performance

The company has performed in accordance with its business plan. ElectraNet's biggest issue is to find capital from shareholders or the market to fund planned capital expenditure. The regulated transmission business is growing organically but is moving into its second 50-year lifecycle and needs substantial asset replacement and upgrading to maintain existing customer service levels. The greatest opportunity for more aggressive growth comes from the unregulated business.

Structure

ElectraNet has three major divisions each led by a General Manager: Finance and Corporate (Service Area); Assets and Operations; and Development and Projects. Finance and Corporate is the support function; Assets and Operations focuses on monitoring and managing the power flows through existing assets; and Development and Projects focuses on developing and building new assets. The focus of the latter two divisions is mainly project and contractual management.

The company's four shareholders are: Powerlink, 41.11% (four directors); YTL Power, 33.5% (three directors); Hastings Fund Management, 19.94% (two directors); and UniSuper, 5.45% (no directors). Each shareholder is entitled to one director for every 10 % of shares held. There is a Board of nine external Directors. There is no permanent Chairman but a rotating Chair is appointed for each meeting. This creates some issues as well as opportunities.

Brand

ElectraNet is a single purpose company with a guaranteed return from the regulator for the regulated business. Hence the company is very much in a dominant, monopolistic position in that area of the market – around 90% of their sales. There are opportunities for achieving growth in the unregulated market related to wind farms and large infrastructure projects.

The company has leased the network from the government for 200 years. Even though the assets will only last for 50 years, there is an obligation to hand back a fully operating network in 2200.

To protect the brand under the licence, ElectraNet must meet standards for reliability, quality, supply and re-investment. ElectraNet's brand is therefore important in the eyes of the State Government, the regulator and its customers. As the company begins to compete for more unregulated business, the brand and what it stands for will become increasingly important.

The core values and behaviours that form "The ElectraNet Way" are:

- Integrity – being ethical, trustworthy, fair and honest.
- Commitment – doing what they say they will do.
- Commercially focused – optimising the balance between risk and reward.
- Customers and other stakeholders – providing outstanding service.
- Focus on outcomes – driving to completion in an efficient manner.
- Continuous improvement – finding innovative solutions.
- Staff – empowering them to take responsibility.

The company is focusing on work force planning, succession planning and a graduate program to ensure that these fundamentals are improved in the business.

Progress of "The ElectraNet Way" is measured by an annual employee opinion survey and monthly performance indicators.

Strategic Issues

ElectraNet's main strategic issues are: ongoing access to significant capital for investment in the grid; a shortage of skilled people to replace an ageing workforce; competition from other electricity infrastructure businesses; funding of the unregulated business; maintaining ElectraNet's financial rating; keeping up to date with new technology; maintaining efficient and effective operating costs; and the future of the existing electricity industry (with its greenhouse effects on the environment) in a low carbon and global warming world.

INSIGHTS INTO

Leading and Managing an Infrastructure Company

Leading and managing an infrastructure company has dimensions that are quite different from other commercial businesses. Most notably the business has to submit five-year revenue applications to a regulatory authority for review and approval. The company has just undertaken a revenue reset project. It aims to achieve a regulated revenue stream to maximise shareholder value and minimise regulatory risks for the 2008-2013 regulatory period and in the longer term, while maintaining customer service levels in an increasingly digital age. The company has created a long-term planning approach called Network 2025, which establishes principles to guide decisions to meet customer and stakeholder needs over the next 20 years. The company must therefore work closely with policy makers, advisers, regulators and other stakeholders to influence regulatory changes to protect and further ElectraNet's commercial position. In a highly politicised, bureaucratic area, this activity is critical.

A capital management strategy is needed to manage ElectraNet's capital structure and debt financing arrangements. Meanwhile, it is important to manage interest rate exposures and maintain acceptable credit rating levels with international credit rating agencies to minimise the cost of capital. In addition, the company needs to provide sustainable, tax effective distributions to shareholders, maintain liquidity, expand the business and have sufficient funds to operate effectively and manage debt.

It is also imperative to have a network and asset management strategy to ensure cost efficiency, functionality and maintenance that includes regional development, asset replacement, and asset refurbishment. Because ElectraNet's business is critical to the functioning of South Australia, risk management and insurance strategies are necessary to achieve an acceptable level of risk, to balance risk and reward, and to protect the business against significant losses.

It is also of critical importance for capital expenditure to be delivered within the regulatory allowance for the current period.

All of these factors mean that the skills for leading and managing this organisation are quite different from other commercial businesses.

Ian Stirling

WHAT ARE THE SECRETS OF YOUR SUCCESS AS A CEO?

The first thing is to have a strategic view of both your industry and where your company is situated in that industry.

Unless you can take a helicopter view of what's going on around you, you almost end up as a Chief Operating Officer (COO). You are running the operation, and in our industry segment the money largely comes in the door no matter what we do. We have to almost force ourselves to have this broader view. But our view can also be a lot more long term.

The thing of which I am most proud is that I brought to this company the idea of "Network Vision 2025". I was taking a long-term view of where we wanted to be. And that's really required a major rethink and review of all our processes in the country. During the 1990s when it was still owned by the state, everyone knew the company didn't have a lot of money. I wasn't here then. But history says we were spending $25 million every year on capital and every one of those dollars was finding the cheapest solution. A number of these decisions were probably sub-optimal and unlikely to deliver the lowest lifetime cost. The legacy of that is a whole lot of different types of equipment. In the long term, issues are not always best dealt with by buying the cheapest piece of equipment.

What does successful CEO thinking take?

I think you have got to step out of your business sometimes, have a look at it from outside and get your clients to assist you with that thinking. Then you must jump back into your business and test to see if there are any shortfalls in the organisation, service offered, or in what we are doing generally.

Successful CEOs need to actually consult their people in a structured format as regularly as they can. Listen to what your people are telling you; listen to what your customers are telling you. Then try to put that together. Grab it from inside, grab it from outside and then adjust the vision.

What are the biggest challenges and opportunities of being a great CEO?

Challenges: Obtaining capital for expansion.

Opportunities: Obtaining highly skilled staff.

What is the one thing, if it could be done, that would have the greatest impact on you as a CEO?

Being able to take the company to the next level. To some extent that would require us to move out of this single focus because the growth opportunities would be substantial.

What has been your biggest disappointment as a CEO?

Inevitably, people leave the company whom you never really wanted to go. Either they couldn't make the transition or they lacked the breadth of skills and attitudes required in the future. It can be very difficult when friendships are involved.

How do you handle rejection and failure?

You have to push through. We all make mistakes.

We must seek to understand why they happen and what can be done about them.

What key decisions have led to your success?

I think I need to refer to the downsizing, which was part of the culture change. It wasn't downsizing for the sake of downsizing, but in order to get the right type of people in the right numbers and to focus on the right things.

How many hours a week do you work?

60 hours per week.

How do you plan?

We need to step back from a short-term network point of view and take a longer-term strategic view. As mentioned earlier, we do this in the context of our 20-year vision. Then we translate that into a document published yearly. This encompasses a 10-year view from which we determine a five-year view and a one-year view. We have also entered into long-term supply arrangements for up to five years with major suppliers.

What are the major factors in your role as a CEO that have helped you, hindered you and blocked change?

Helped you: My experience. I have been in the industry a long time so I understand the regulatory arrangements almost but not quite as well as our regulatory manager.

Hindered you: I don't think I could really say a lot of things have got in the way but opportunities need to exist at the right time.

Blocked change: Hierarchies and old paradigms.

How and when have you transitioned your role?

When I became CEO in 2002.

What is your succession plan?

We have a long term plan to bring a number of my direct reports up to CEO potential.

What is your exit strategy?

When I reach around 60 I plan to retire from this role but stay active in business.

What is business success to you?

Achieving stretch goals and delivering for both owners and customers.

What problems do you, as a CEO, talk about on a day-to-day basis?

Operational problems, staffing and people issues, and business opportunities. They would comprise 80% of discussions that take place.

What are the issues that you have to deal with in your leadership role as a CEO?

Bringing people along at a fast enough pace. There is always a tension between what needs to be achieved and what people can do.

How has individual and group mentoring helped you?

I have had various mentors. They give you insights that you can't really learn any other way.

What changes have you observed in the workplace culture to remain competitive to employ Generation Y?

Generation Y is a real issue for us going forward. We have certainly made a lot of changes as part of the whole shift to make the culture more flexible. Everyone comments on how family supportive we are but we also say, don't forget that it is also a performance culture. We are happy to give staff freedom to the extent they can prove their need.

Do you have to sacrifice your own life and family to be successful in business? Any comments?

I don't think it is mandatory. It can happen at times. Everyone needs to do work related things sometimes and therefore lose other opportunities and outside experiences. I definitely wouldn't say you can only be A or B.

How have you capitalised on your business and developed it in an extraordinary way, geometrically?

I don't think I could say that I have done that as yet. Success is a never-ending journey but we are focusing on ensuring that our people are empowered to fully deliver for customers and that we will achieve sustained high growth by leveraging our balance sheet, our people and our IP. We are still in the throes of preparation.

How has your development as a leader maximised your impact on all of the stakeholders you work with?

I provide leadership in a variety of ways. I am a very situational leader but integrity and honesty are my two primary drivers. After all, I have to live, firstly, with myself.

How has your life developed to make you a better person and how have you maximised this?

I had the goal to be a CEO and I am grateful that I have achieved it. I believe I have influenced and helped a lot of people and even though there have been some personal costs for me, I have grasped each new challenge.

Lessons you have Learned as a CEO

Act as an adviser/mentor to your senior management team.

Provide positive leadership.

Trust your people.

Understand that your people know more than you will ever know.

Make sure that you have processes that allow flexibility.

One size does not fit all.

Always look to the long term but never forget profit is for today and tomorrow.

Learn to serve multiple masters.

Work with your Board and not against them. Always remember that they are the owners; it's their way.

Change your culture by downsizing the company.

Push forward with the re-growth of any company by aggressively looking at new business opportunities.

Ian Stirling

Final Word

Do what you think is right and give everyone the opportunity to reach their zenith.

Questions for Contemplation

Reflect on your life and Ian's experiences:

1. Are you satisfied that you have been the best you can be in your circumstances, both from a business and personal perspective? If not, what do you need to change?

2. What challenges and opportunities do you need to focus on and take action on?

3. How do you need to grow in serving multiple masters?

4. What does it mean to be a positive leader?

Favorite Book

Competitive Strategy: Techniques for Analyzing Industries and Competitors, by Michael E Porter

Contact Details

Ian Stirling

CEO

ElectraNet Pty Ltd

Email: stirling.ian@electranet.com.au

Website: www.electranet.com.au

Opera

3. Operating a Family Business

John

Establishing a Dynasty – One Winery, Five Generations

If you inherited a three-generation company, how would you lead it and grow it?

John Angove

Born: 1947

Education: Year 12, St Peter's College, Adelaide; Bachelor of Science (Organic Chemistry and Microbiology), University of Adelaide, 1966-68; Graduate Diploma, Commerce, South Australian Institute of Technology, 1969.

Career: Wine industry experience in the UK, Europe and USA 1970-71; sales and marketing in Renmark, South Australia, 1971-82; Managing Director of Angove's in 1983; Chairman of Angove's in 2001.

Personal: John enjoys aviation, golf, water and snow skiing, classical music and spending time with his family.

> "Nothing worthwhile is easy, but with persistence, support and trust in others, almost anything is achievable."

Background

Dr William Thomas Angove founded Angove's in 1886, after he and his young family emigrated from Cornwall to Tea Tree Gully in the foothills of Adelaide. Dr Angove's active interest in chemistry led him to experiment with winemaking and viticulture. He first produced fortified wines for his patients but soon found a growing customer base that turned his hobby into a business.

Thomas Angove, a descendant of the founder, steered the company from a small-hobby business to a winery of substance, producing a diverse range of wine styles for local and export markets. It was his son, Thomas William Carlyon Angove, whose foresight, leadership and passion shaped the future of the company and the South Australian wine industry.

A graduate in oenology (the study of wine), Thomas joined the family business after serving as a pilot during World War II. In 1965, after several years of experimentation, he invented the "bag in box" or cask package for wine, a world-first that revolutionised wine sales internationally. Under Thomas's guidance, Angove's pioneered the vineyard and trellising techniques that allowed future mechanical harvesting, once again leading the way in the wine industry.

Thomas's son, John, first began working in the business during school vacations. After completing a science degree and post-graduate studies in commerce, he worked overseas in the wine industry in Europe and the USA before returning home to develop a national network of branches as Sales and Marketing Manager.

John then assisted his father before rising to the position of Managing Director in 1983. Thomas retired from the Board due to ill health in 2001 and John was appointed Chairman.

Angove's celebrated its 120th anniversary in 2006 with 170 employees at six locations and with sales of $48.9 million.

This dynamic family winery, which has spanned the turn of two centuries and withstood two world wars, floods and fires, is now in the midst of its most amazing growth phase ever. It is Australia's eleventh largest winery by branded sales and is the eighth largest exporter in the industry. As John Angove says, "We are extremely proud of what we have achieved over the past 120 years. To reach this milestone is a credit to all the hard work of the people within our company, our loyal suppliers and business partners and, of course, our valued customers".

Products and Services

Angove's products include: St Agnes Brandy; Stone's Ginger Wine; a comprehensive spread of fine wines including the Vineyard Select range made from grapes sourced from the Coonawarra region, McLaren Vale, the Clare Valley and the Adelaide Hills; the Long Row range; and fortified wines. The company also represents Australian and imported wines from a range of premium producers.

Growth Trends

Despite the propensity for oversupply in the wine industry, John Angove believes the outlook for the industry and the company is very strong. Angove's wines are enjoying excellent reviews and brands such as Stone's Ginger Wine and St Agnes Brandy continue to dominate their categories. In fact, the St Agnes label has further strengthened its popularity by moving beyond brandy into grape-based vodka.

The company's association with Trinchero Family Estates in the USA has been a great move forward. The development of this relationship was aided by the fact that both companies hold traditional family values very dear. Sales to the USA in the past year have grown strongly and this new joint venture to distribute Angove's premium wines will help build momentum considerably.

The domestic market for the winery has remained steady despite an increasingly competitive environment. Angove's is setting its sights on $100 million annual turnover by 2015. As John Angove says, "One of our strengths as a privately owned company is our ability to plan long-term without having to appeal to share market analysts. We have a relative amount of freedom".

Another significant growth factor has been the redevelopment of the 1,200-acre Nanya Vineyard that is half way through a 12 year, $10 million program aimed at underpinning export growth and improving efficiency, water conservation and, ultimately, grape and wine quality. Nanya is now at the leading edge of vineyard practices after a move to computer-controlled drip irrigation, vertical trellising and a 90-degree change in direction of the rows from north-south to east-west. This will assist with mechanical harvesting, reduce frost risk and deliver major savings on water use. The company has also expanded its bottling capacity in recent years and provides contract bottling services for other winemakers.

Performance

Angove's performance over the years has been solid and reliable; some wineries don't stay in business long enough to get cobwebs in the cellars! Only a select few reach the "100 Plus Club" – reserved for wineries that have survived a century or more.

In Angove's case, the secret to longevity has been patience, innovation, vision, passion, a willingness to plough money back into the business, great people, consistently good and affordable products, and recognising the importance of branding. Angove's has also experienced the industry's cycles many times and brings wisdom and a level head to these situations, as well as a long-term international view.

Perhaps the most important reason for Angove's success is their core value of loyalty – a sustainable long-term commitment to consumers, growers, staff and business partners. With the proliferation of brands vying for the consumer dollar, Angove's believes that it is critical to be loyal to their national and international customers. They do this by consistently delivering high quality wines produced from superior grapes.

Angove's is committed to keeping a long-term focus and to preserving strong relations with growers to develop a sustainable industry. The company is just as dedicated to its staff and vice versa; a fact demonstrated by the large number of long-term employees.

Loyalty also applies to business partners, such as Collotype Labels. Another family business, this company has had the printing contract for St Agnes Brandy labels for over 70 years. Collotype's Chairman, Peter Teakle, says, "Our families have enjoyed a unique relationship that has extended beyond business and we see it continuing for generations to come". Peter's father, was, in fact, cremated with a collection of St Agnes Brandy labels in his coffin!

Angove's has been outstanding in the export arena and is one of the biggest exporters of branded wine. Exports currently represent 45% of Angove's total business and are expected to grow in the next few years to account for more than 60% of its turnover. Angove's exports to 30 countries with key markets in the US, UK, Denmark and Canada.

In the tight UK wine market, Australian wineries are seeking competitive advantages. The British Retail Consortium (BRC) Certification is the standard used by all of the major UK supermarkets as the benchmark for food safety, hygiene and quality standards. In 2004, Angove's became the first Australian winery to achieve this highest level of quality certification.

To further consolidate their global position, Angove's is looking to secure a foothold in non-traditional wine markets such as Sri Lanka, India, China, Vietnam, Brazil, Kenya, Israel and the Philippines. As Victoria Angove, the company's International Business Development Manager, says, "When growth slows in mature global markets we need to be well placed to turn to non-traditional regions".

Structure

The company is governed by a Board of six people, including an external Non-Executive Director. The rest of the Board comprises: John Angove as Chairman; Victoria Angove as International Business Development Manager; a Finance and Administration Manager; a

Sales and Marketing Manager; and a Purchasing and Packaging Manager.

John Angove has six direct reports: the Human Resource Manager, the Chief Winemaker, the Purchasing and Packaging Manager, the Operations Manager, the Sales and Marketing Manager, and the Finance and Administration Manager. Most of the staff is located at the main production facility in Renmark. There is a national sales and marketing office at the former Tea Tree Gully winery and there are sales offices in every mainland state.

Brand

Angove's challenge is to keep building brands with market strength rather than just anonymous bottles of wine. As a family company facing a "brand battlefield" in Australia and overseas, Angove's is executing a brand strategy that incorporates marketing, advertising and public relations through the promotion of "Brand Angove's" – synonymous with family values, quality wine and a modern approach. Over the past five years, Angove's has focused on creating truly global brands that are transferable between different international markets.

Sponsorship has also been key in developing Angove's brands. Last year, Angove's added Bowls Australia and the Adelaide International Horse Trials to its list of sponsorships, to capitalise on the growth of these sports in Australia. Sponsorships of other sporting organisations have been strategically selected in line with the winery's target market. Angove's has also used cause-related marketing as a component of their branding strategy. Angove's Bear Crossing label supports the Australian Koala Foundation; every bottle of this product sold around the world contributes to saving one of Australia's icons, with over $300,000 raised to date.

Strategic Issues

The most important issues facing Angove's today include: government taxation; water quality and supply; oversupply of grapes; reliance on export for future development, particularly when the Australian dollar strengthens; being a capital intensive industry with low return on investment; concentration of ownership in Australia at the retail level; increasing net margins by reducing costs and increasing efficiency; and continually redeveloping the brand to increase the top-line revenue to cover national infrastructure costs.

INSIGHTS INTO

The old adage that the first generation builds a business, the second grows it and the third loses it is of real concern. With a history spanning five generations, Angove's is one of Australia's oldest surviving family-owned wineries and living proof of how careful succession planning can provide long-lasting benefits. Not only must owners take responsibility for running their business but also for safe guarding the family legacy. As John Angove says, "I remember when our children were growing up, my approach to work changed completely. There was an awakening of the significance of the company to the family and a sudden awareness of my responsibility to maintain the company for future generations. Without the family continuity, it might have been tempting to build up the business and sell it".

John became Managing Director at 35 but only assumed complete control when he was 54 years old. Conceivably, he may have felt that his father, who stepped down from the Board at 84, should have relinquished control at an earlier age. This indeed is a real trap for family businesses – when should the old make way for the new and how long should the transition take? There are advantages and drawbacks with any decision like this so it is important to have wise external mentors to help guide you through this dangerous period. The decision must be made at the right time, and for the benefit of the company, the current generation and the future generation.

With only a few family members involved in the company there is less potential for conflict. As John says, "The lineage has been very thin and there has only been in each generation one male member prepared to continue involvement in the business. My father was an only son and I am the only son to continue in this business".

However, it is John's eldest daughter, Victoria, who is being groomed as a potential successor. Victoria is commercially orientated and developed a passion for the business at an early age. "There have been no free rides along the way. In fact, I think that being part of the family brings with it certain expectations and a real need to ensure that I am a positive contributor to the company. I've relished every opportunity to learn and be involved, from lugging massive wine barrels during vintage to liaising with distributors overseas."

John's son, Richard, has worked as a winemaker in many parts of the world. He previously worked for Angove's as a cellar hand, in bottling, in the laboratory and in the vineyard and plans to rejoin the family company sometime in the future. He will, with Victoria, carry the responsibility for the family company.

While John has no immediate thoughts of retirement, ensuring the long-term future of his family's company remains top of mind. Angove's has always encouraged its family members to pursue other interests and careers before deciding whether they wanted to be involved in the business long-term. John believes that "...this is one of the secrets of Angove's success. Not only does this bring to the company benefits of outside experience and knowledge, it also ensures that the family members who come back are fully committed to the cause. If they do decide to join the business, we believe it's vitally important to teach them the ropes from the ground up so they acquire a critical understanding of every part of the business".

WHAT ARE THE SECRETS OF YOUR SUCCESS AS A CEO?

> Being open, communicative and a good listener. Not being dogmatic. Being willing to listen to people who know more about the subject than I do.

What does successful CEO thinking take?

Taking time out to think in a peaceful environment. Sometimes it's on the golf course, sometimes it's just sitting in the chair after Sunday lunch.

What are the biggest challenges and opportunities of being a great CEO?

Challenges: Making sure that the business keeps on working successfully – the buck stops with you and there are so many moving parts in the mechanism.

Opportunities: Delegate as much as you can with trust but oversee what's happening.

What is the one thing, if it could be done, that would have the greatest impact on you as a CEO?

Better communication. I like to know what's happening – I don't want to interfere, I just want to know! It's not lust for power; it's greed for information.

What has been your biggest disappointment as a CEO?

Losing key staff is always a great disappointment, but such changes always bring with them new opportunity.

What key decisions have led to your success?

Developing the management team and committing to the vineyard re-development. We didn't know at the time that it was as smart as it was, but what a great time to have a vineyard out of production!

Also, the rejuvenation of the production facility has been a key decision (due to the current oversupply of grapes).

How many hours a week do you work?

45 – I manage that quite well. But I don't count my "weekend reading time" in that.

How do you plan?

A diary going forward, and daily, dare I say, hand-to-mouth. I'm not a great planner. I have a list of things that have got to happen, but then I'll arrive at work and suddenly someone's at the door with an important issue I must make time for.

What are the major factors in your role as a CEO that have helped you, hindered you and blocked change?

Helped you: My personality, openness and willingness to listen – people skills.

Hindered you: Procrastination.

Blocked change: Being risk averse.

What part has innovation played in your company?

From a production point of view, huge. We are a technology and science-based industry and need to keep ahead of the game.

How and when have you transitioned your role?

My father's exit as Chairman was a big factor. I cannot believe the transition that it's been and the change that it made in my life.

What is your succession plan?

It's evolving as time goes by. I've got at least another six or seven years as CEO. Victoria currently has a key role in marketing. Richard, my son, has a vision of continuing to work elsewhere for a while as a winemaker, rejoining the company in due course as the key family member at the production end of the business. Sophie, my other daughter, is a teacher focusing on children with disabilities.

What is your exit strategy?

I will continue as Chairman until I'm comfortable that Victoria and Richard have got the management of the company under control. I see Richard being in charge of production and Victoria being in charge of the commercial, sales and marketing side. I'm very sensitive to the problems that I went through, but I think I have a different relationship with Victoria and Richard than I had with my father. Always in mind is that planning and reality often have different courses!

What is business success to you?

It's the comfort in knowing that I have succeeded in ensuring the family company continues to prosper. I'm not hungry for money; that's not a driver at all.

What problems do you, as a CEO, talk about on a day-to-day basis?

People issues, sales, technology, environmental issues and government regulations.

What are the issues that you have to deal with in your leadership role as a CEO?

Not being sufficiently definite and not deciding quickly enough.

How has individual and group mentoring helped you?

Enormously, by giving me new ideas and making me accountable to take action.

What changes have you observed in the workplace culture to remain competitive to employ Generation Y?

I'm not sure that we've got many of them at the moment. That's perhaps an issue as the key people we have in key roles get older. We're a very old company, but I do think we continue to develop a young "can do" personality.

What impact has the business had on your life?

It has been my life and I have benefited enormously.

Do you have to sacrifice your own life and family to be successful in business?

I did in the early days with travel demands and work demands. Claire was at home struggling with the children and I was in Europe and America. Now there are still things that I don't have enough time for – golf, playing the piano – but if I'm putting eight hours of work in each day, it's because I want to.

How have you capitalised on your business and developed it in an extraordinary way, geometrically?

The right people are doing it, and I provide the fine-tuning along the way to retain the right direction.

How has your development as a leader maximised your impact on all of the stakeholders you work with?

It is like piloting an aircraft. The CEO needs to adjust the trim tabs in a company so that it flies with maximum efficiency, correcting the direction as needed and providing that gentle urging.

How has your life developed to make you a better person and how have you maximised this?

Resolving the issues of the succession period that my father and I went through has made me a better person and allowed me to maximise what I've been doing. It was a difficult time for us both, but the end result has been successful so one could say we were both right. The experiences of life provide endless learning opportunities; the trick is to take on the learning with enthusiasm and commitment.

Lessons you have Learned as a CEO

Get the right people in the right slots.

Don't procrastinate when the people are wrong. Fire quickly, hire slowly.

Treat risk with respect.

Spend capital slowly – there's always tomorrow.

Support good employees.

Remember the importance of people skills, in self and others – emotional intelligence.

Don't be afraid to seek advice and say, "I don't know".

Be approachable, have an open door policy and be easy to contact.

Expect mistakes and accept mistakes. It's part of learning.

Don't be a one-man band; be inclusive.

Don't be obsessed with planning.

Exploit major export markets and try and win a major contract overseas. It will help you leapfrog the competition and penetrate the global market.

Having the right quality management team operating and integrated is critical.

The marketing and sales functions are the most critical in business.

Love and respect those around you and you will get love and respect in return. Tolerance is a great strength to develop.

Balance in life is what fits you, not what others think should fit you.

Final Word

Learn from life's experiences, and use the lessons learned to better the way forward.

Questions for Contemplation

As you reflect on John's life, ask yourself:

1. How do you relate to people? How open and accessible are you?

2. How open are you to the ideas of others?

3. How do you handle major difficulties that are, to a large degree, outside of your control?

4. How well are you able to deal with family members in your own business?

Favorite Books

The 7 Habits of Highly Effective People, by Stephen Covey

The Bonfire of the Vanities, by Tom Wolfe

Contact Details

John Angove

Chairman and CEO

Angove's Pty Ltd

Email: john.angove@angoves.com.au

Website: www.angoves.com.au

Roger

Systematic Growth in the Grocery Business

What would you do to take a small corner grocery store and turn it into a large company?

Roger Drake

Born: 1948

Education: Gilles Plains High School – Matriculation

Career: Trainee Manager and Store Manager, Coles Myer Group, 1965; opened his first supermarket in 1974 – a three-lane store at Mitcham, South Australia; currently Managing Director of Drake Foodmarkets, a leading independent retailer with 46 stores across South Australia and Queensland.

Personal: Roger is interested in travelling, golf, water and snow skiing and sports in general.

"The most important lesson that I have learned in business is to be humble and don't let ego get in the way of good business sense. I have always been and always will be just a simple grocer."

Background

In 1965, Roger Drake commenced his supermarket retailing career with the Coles Myer Group. Ironically, he was initially rejected by Woolworths, who felt that he was unsuitable for a career in retail! In 1974, after 9 years with Coles Myer, Roger established his own business by purchasing his first store for $29,000 in Mitcham, a southern suburb of Adelaide – a three-lane supermarket called Jack and Jill's. After three successful years, Roger opened a larger supermarket at Torrensville. The company has grown opportunistically since then and now owns 46 stores throughout South Australia and Queensland, with a turnover of almost $560 million, approximately $230 million of that being from Queensland.

Products and Services

Drake Foodmarkets is the largest independent grocery retailer in Australia and specialises in supermarket retailing. In addition, the company operates a liquor store, several news agencies and a consulting service – Select Professional Retail Services. The company also has a significant property portfolio.

Growth Trends

Drake Foodmarkets grew slowly at first but accelerated this growth through opportunistic acquisition of stores that were for sale, or through opening new supermarkets in shopping centre developments. "Whether I acquired a store or started a store, the process was the same after refits and upgrades – three to four years of losses, then profit. I would then commence the process again with another store."

The company had a number of stages to its growth including the acquisition of eight David stores, the acquisition of five big stores from the failed Franklin group, the acquisition of six stores in South Eastern Queensland between August and October in 2004, and the acquisition of five stores from Metcash in September 2006. The Drake Foodmarkets company is now the third largest grocery retailer in South Australia after Woolworths and Coles Myer. The company now has 35 stores in South Australia including 29 Foodland stores, one Drake Foodmarket store, four news agencies, and a liquor store at Wallaroo. In Queensland, 11 stores trade under the banner of Drake Super IGA stores. The company now employs 4,300 staff – 3,200 of whom are based in South Australia. Drake Foodmarkets expects to have more than 60 stores in the next five years through expanding its existing markets in Queensland and South Australia. The next growth targets will be northern New South Wales, the Northern Territory and Western Australia.

Performance

One of the biggest issues facing the supermarket retailing industry is the dominance of Woolworths and Coles Myer. These supermarket giants have had a huge impact on independent retailers in this sector. Gradually, the "Big Two" have acquired more and more stores, as well as expanding into petrol and liquor, with attractive discounting of petrol based on a minimum grocery spend. No independent retailer can match the market penetration and buying power of these two major retailers, which have 80% of the grocery market in Australia. This is the environment in which Drake Foodmarkets has had to perform, grow and compete on price, service and range. Despite this, the company has grown significantly thanks to Roger Drake's vision – taking calculated risks supporting major supply groups and maintaining a careful approach to acquisitions, which has seen Drake Foodmarkets become a significant competitor to the "Big Two".

Through an experienced management team of long-term employees, every acquisition was tested against a model to ensure that the stores being purchased would perform after upgrades, refits and an increase in product range. Of crucial importance were the management of each store and the creation of the "Drake culture" focusing on outstanding customer service. There have also been 1-2 marginal stores, including a hardware store, which are a reminder of the need to use intuition as well as the projection model.

Roger Drake and his management team regularly travel overseas to investigate innovation, industry trends and worldwide best practice standards. In fact, in terms of benchmarking, Drake Foodmarkets take their cues from a company outside of Australia, setting their performance against a leading US independent retail chain by the name of Wegman's.

Drake Foodmarkets has had extraordinary results and has been highly awarded in the business sector with a range of national and international awards including:

1997:   IGA Australian Retailer of the Year for the Woodcroft Foodland store

1998:   IGA International Retailer of the Year for the Woodcroft Foodland store

2003:   Roger Drake – Master Entrepreneur of the Year

As the company has grown it has invested in technology systems to ensure ongoing high performance. It has not been an initiator of trends like Internet shopping, preferring to follow the competition's lead. This has allowed Drake Foodmarkets to observe the latest technology trends without the need for immediate capital investment or risk. Once a trend is successfully established in the marketplace, the company can then embrace and improve upon that technology.

Structure

The company is governed by a Board consisting of the CEO and two external long-term directors. The structure is made up of a General Manager, a Financial Controller, an Operations Manager, a Loss Preventions Manager, a Marketing Manager, a Human Resource Manager and a Business Systems/Administration Manager. The Queensland operation is managed by Roger's son, John-Paul Drake, who reports to the General Manager. Individual stores are managed by Store Managers who report to one of five Store Supervisors. A comprehensive head office in Torrensville, South Australia, provides administration, accounting and information technology support.

Succession is a critical issue for such a large organisation. Promotion generally occurs from within for several reasons: as a career path opportunity for staff; because of commitment to the Drake culture; and because staff performance and chemistry with management is an already known factor. Early identification of talented staff is undertaken for accelerated training and development. Of particular importance is the fact that Roger's wife and three children work in the business. They are all committed to seeing the business continue for the coming generations and to take roles in the company according the their competence and experience. Roger is equally committed to building the Drake dynasty and seeing the family business flourish well into the future.

Brand

The Drake Foodmarkets brand is focused on price, range, quality, customer service, niche marketing, modern facilities, and well trained and presented staff. Customer service and quality are the major passions of the organisation and this is prevalent in the attitude of staff and the satisfied feedback from customers. Whenever a new store is acquired, it is immediately refitted and upgraded in keeping with the brand's image, and the variety of products available is increased to be in keeping with other Drake Foodmarkets stores.

Strategic Issues

The major issues confronting the company arise out of the dominance of the industry by the duopoly of Woolworths and Coles, who are now extending their range to include retail wine sales and petrol outlets. This makes it very difficult for smaller operations to compete. Also of great concern is the commitment of both major players to sell their own "home" brand products; this places many quality Australian goods under threat and will impact on smaller retailers in the industry by potentially limiting the availability and range of products they will be able to sell, as well as affecting the price-points of these goods.

INSIGHTS INTO

Roger Drake is a shrewd, humble, simple grocer – and a visionary leader. He passionately leads by example and never gives up. He accepts that he is only good at a few things and surrounds himself with a winning team who complement his abilities. His focus is on health, happiness and wealth, in that order. He dreams big and keeps on enlarging his thinking. To him, everything is a possibility and nothing is impossible. This is the fundamental reason for the success of his company.

In addition is his simple, straightforward approach to running a business. He does not overcomplicate things and always has the fundamentals at his fingertips – bank balances, sales, wages and costs. He still visits stores every week and manages by walking around – he really knows retailing and his customers. He passionately believes that customers are the life-blood of his company and he is passionate about exceeding their expectations.

He believes that it is important to position the business in a strategic way and have a consistent brand image for all stores. His company vision and strategy is about taking calculated risks, supporting major suppliers and having a carefully tested and proven model for opportunistic acquisition of stores.

He has created a caring, family relationship and atmosphere in his company and set up an environment of learning to enable everyone in the business to grow through training, education and development. As a result, the business grows. Staff take pride in being Drake employees.

In short, Roger Drake has built a large and successful business through implementing a range of simple, elegant practices centred on personal learning.

WHAT ARE THE SECRETS OF YOUR SUCCESS AS A CEO?

Surround yourself with the right people. Do not over-complicate things. Have the fundamental drivers at your fingertips on a daily basis – the bank balance, the sales, the wages, the costs and the key things that make your business successful.

What does successful CEO thinking take?

Common sense and accepting that you are only good at a few things. Don't be frightened to use the resources of other people that are smarter than you. You listen, you learn and you make a decision, but ultimately you are the one who's got to make that decision. At the end of the day, it's your business.

What are the biggest challenges and opportunities of being a great CEO?

Do not let your ego get in the way and think that you are good at a whole range of things.

What is the one thing, if it could be done, that would have the greatest impact on you as a CEO?

I would like better time management skills. I try and cram too much into the day. You have got to have the right people around you to delegate some of the things you do.

What has been your biggest disappointment as a CEO?

Spending too much time on the business over the past 32 years.

How do you handle rejection and failure?

Probably not well. No one likes to fail. My biggest failure was in the hardware store and not being able to turn that around. We leave making the tough decisions to last. At least the glass is always full because I'm an optimistic person.

What key decisions have led to your success?

Firstly, having a sign in the store: "Rule #1 – the customer is always right; Rule #2 – if the customer is ever wrong, refer to Rule #1". Secondly, developing a great management team.

How many hours a week do you work?

Probably 55-60. In the early days it was whatever it took – seven days a week.

How do you plan?

I am a great believer in goal setting – yearly, 5-year and 10-year goals. Dream big dreams. I don't think anything is totally impossible if you really put your mind to it and work around it.

What are the major factors in your role as a CEO that have helped you, hindered you and blocked change?

Helped you: Persistence

Hindered you: Conservatism. I'll take calculated risk as opposed to uncalculated risk.

Blocked change: Being too conservative.

What part has innovation played in your company?

I've been a follower. I want to be at the leading edge not the bleeding edge! Let Coles and Woolworths do all the way-out stuff; I pick their good ideas and make them better.

How and when have you transitioned your role?

It's been over time. Getting the General Manager in place and then, in turn, getting the people around him was a major transition in my role. I also have identified people with talent and tried to fast track them.

What is your succession plan?

Obviously we have a succession plan to identify people to move up. My son, John-Paul, is there, but he is only there if he is good enough – he accepts that mantle. And if he's not good enough then I am sure there are plenty of other people who could step up.

What is your exit strategy?

Probably to Executive Chairman at a point in time when I find that the energy level required to run the business is not within me.

What is business success to you?

A fantastic journey.

What problems do you, as a CEO, talk about on a day-to-day basis?

Mainly people.

What are the issues that you have to deal with in your leadership role as a CEO?

Mainly people.

How do you allow the space and time for creative thinking for yourself and your staff?

I have my quiet place. I have a place that I can go, to get some quiet time in my own mind, because I am a dreamer – it's an island in the sky.

How has individual and group mentoring helped you?

I need somebody to keep me on track (I think most people do), whether that's through a group situation or with a mentor. I think it is important to have somebody that will tell it as it is, as opposed to how you would like it to be.

What changes have you observed in the workplace culture to remain competitive to employ Generation Y?

We have noticed, like most other businesses, an obsession towards less hours and linking that with lifestyle. It's not about money with these people; it is about quality of life.

What impact has the business had on your life?

It's been a remarkable journey considering where I came from to where I am now, and where I see I will be in the future. I have been given opportunities that I could not have ever comprehended.

Do you have to sacrifice your own life and family to be successful in business? Any comments?

If you are smarter than me it could be done. But I didn't because I wasn't that smart. Other people might be able to do it differently. I had to start, grow and establish a business and that is a tough road.

How have you capitalised on your business

and developed it in an extraordinary way, geometrically?

I think it is continual growth through using systems that you develop and then taking the stretch when the opportunities are available.

How has your development as a leader maximised your impact on all of the stakeholders you work with?

Taking an interest in other people and managing by walking around every store regularly, as this is a hands-on business – I am a simple grocer.

How has your life developed to make you a better person and how have you maximised this?

By promoting other people and by looking after people who work for us, to give them the opportunities that life has given me; opportunities that probably not even they would have dreamed possible.

Lessons you have Learned as a CEO

Rule #1 – the customer is always right; Rule #2 – if the customer is ever wrong, refer to Rule #1.

Customers are the life-blood of the business so invest time in getting to know them and their family.

Provide excellent customer service to them and be passionate about them because in the end they pay your wages.

Exceed your customers' expectations by providing great personal service.

Be passionate about your business.

Never give up.

Associate with other leaders to challenge and sharpen your thinking.

Lead by example and set goals.

Dream dreams and always keep enlarging your thinking.

Never be superior to the team.

Be humble and don't let ego get in the way of good business service.

Get a mentor and good external advisers.

Success has a cost. There is no such thing as a free lunch.

Nothing is impossible if you dream it and chase it.

Be seen as a person with enormous enthusiasm, energy and strategic vision.

Be conservative but also take calculated risks.

Surround yourself with good people.

Make sure that you've got a combination of skills in your team.

Have a "good guy, bad guy" relationship within the organisation – for example, the CEO and the General Manager.

Set up an environment of learning to enable everyone in the business to grow.

Lessons you have Learned as a CEO

Enable your people to become better than you through training, education and development.

Create a caring family atmosphere.

Expect that they will make mistakes.

Take your top team overseas every 1-2 years to learn about innovation, industry trends and best practice.

Ensure that you position the business and its brand in a strategic way.

Be a niche operation or dominate the market. Never take a middle position by being either big or small, because competitors from both ends can pick you off.

When growing your company through acquisitions, utilise a model that will determine whether the store will be successful or not.

Run your company by continuously improving processes and systems for all aspects of the business, to ensure consistency and success.

Benchmark your company against the best in the world.

Focus on HHW in that order – Health, Happiness and Wealth.

Final Word

Live your life well, laugh often, love much, always look for the best in others and give them the best that you've got. Be a great parent and love life to the maximum.

Questions for Contemplation

Success like this is also possible for you. Take some time to consider the following questions:

1. What similarities are there between Roger's story and yours?

2. Part of the secret of Roger's success was risk taking. What's stopping you from taking a risk in your life?

3. Where are you now? Where do you want to be? What goals and objectives are you going to set for your future?

4. If you took the risk and lost everything, what is the worst thing that would happen?

Favorite Book

Psychology of Winning, by Denis Waitley

Contact Details

Mr Roger Drake - Managing Director

Drake Foodmarkets

Email: roger.drake@drakefoodmarkets.com.au

Website: www.drakefoodmarkets.com.au

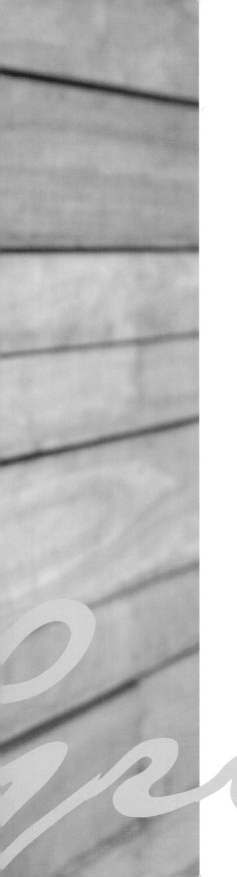

Developing a Successful Niche Business

How would you turn a business into a lifestyle?

Joe Grilli

Born: 1959

Education: Matriculation, Gawler High School, 1975; Bachelor of Applied Science in Oenology (Dux), Roseworthy Agricultural College, 1979; E-Myth Mastery Program 1998-2002.

Career: Cellar Hand and Laboratory Assistant, Angle Vale Vineyards, January-December 1976; Proprietor, CEO and Winemaker of Primo Estate Winery, 1978-Current; Vintage Worker, Chateau Canon, St Emilion, France, September-October 1987; Winemaking Consultancy for Hardy Wine Co. in Umbria, Italy September-November, 1991 and 1992.

Personal: Joe enjoys spending time with his family, and is fond of the finer things in life: good food and wine, travel, cars and motor sports.

"I was the classic technician when I was thrown into the CEO role in 1986 and I struggled on until 1998 when I had a paradigm shift and re-engineered the company through the E-Myth Mastery Course and personal coaching. The company changed immediately, but it took four years to complete the change."

Background

Joe Grilli grew up on his family's horticultural property and, as a child, assisted his parents with growing vegetables, and planting and operating a vineyard. In 1978, while studying Oenology at Roseworthy Agricultural College, Joe started Primo Estate Wines with the help of his parents and his brother. After his marriage to Dina in 1986, Joe and his new wife purchased all the company shares. This was a major step for a traditional Italian family; it was not common for a son to pursue his own dreams instead of his family's direction. However, it was quite clear that it would have been very difficult to accommodate all the differences of opinion within the family, so Primo Estate moved forward under the joint leadership of Joe and Dina Grilli.

Products and Services

Primo Estate makes an exclusive range of unique, handcrafted premium wines, extra virgin olive oils and vinegar under two brands – the Primo Estate and Joseph labels. These products are a reflection of Joe's primary aim – to be creative and to connect with the wonder and magic of the universe.

Growth Trends

From its inception, the company has grown steadily from year to year based on organic compound growth. The fact that it is an industry that is both cyclical and long-term has placed massive demands on capital. Primo Estate grew as cash flow and borrowings would allow, but in a reasonably conservative manner.

There were a few major developments that helped accelerate this growth. Firstly, the development of a more up-market brand (the Joseph brand) that gave the company a new profile. Secondly, a vineyard at Clarendon, south of Adelaide, that provided an alternative source of grapes for the Virginia production facility north of Adelaide. This was an important strategic move to diversify the range and quality of wine which could be produced and therefore change the company image. Thirdly, in 1999, Primo Estate was re-branded to reflect a more Italian style. And, lastly, the company opened a superb new $2 million facility in McLaren Vale in November 2006.

Another major factor (and a significant breakthrough) was the extensive change in management and leadership culture. In 1998, the company was re-engineered from a classic, family-run business to a professionally managed company. As Joe says, "Dina and I were running the company by the seat of our pants until a proper structure was put in place". As a result of the changes, the company grew from a sales turnover of $1.4 million in 1998 to $3.6 million in 2006, more than doubling in eight years. Not only that, but the company now exudes a spirit of excellence in everything it does.

Their products are marketed nationally through agents and internationally through representatives in the UK, USA, Singapore, Japan, New Zealand, Canada and Central Europe.

Primo Estate enjoys solid growth during industry boom times but shows its strength during cyclical downturns. It is during these periods that Primo Estate tends to grow significantly because of long-term thinking and a conservative management style.

Performance

The performance of Primo Estate has been good. With the vineyards in Virginia, Clarendon and McLaren Vale, the olive grove in Virginia, the winery at Virginia, and vinegar making and fortified wine ageing also at Virginia, the company has built a foundation and infrastructure to rise to the next level. Profit margins have grown and annual sales have exceeded the targeted annual growth rate of 15%. The results of the first few months' sales from the new cellar door at McLaren Vale have far exceeded expectations.

The development of the classic, elegant packaging for all of the products, together with the superb contents, has proved to be irresistible to wine and food lovers who appreciate quality and beauty. Add to this the blending of Dina and Joe's Italian heritage with modern Australian winemaking techniques and you end up with a range of exquisite, high-performing products that have been recognised, written up and judged very highly by industry writers, judges and experts.

In tandem with product performance is the experience that customers enjoy at Primo Estate. Undoubtedly, it is a special pleasure to visit the cellar door – the staff are knowledgeable, passionate and professional and the environment is stunning. Satisfaction and a sense of enjoyment are at the heart of Primo Estate and are a direct reflection of Joe and Dina Grilli's values.

One cannot help but be impressed by the clean, well-organised winery at the Virginia vineyard and the clever use of old and new technology. All of the vineyards are managed in sympathy with the environment using techniques such as minimum chemical usage and minimum cultivation to produce the best quality fruit possible.

Structure

The company has two equal shareholders (Dina and Joe Grilli) who are the only Directors. An external mentor assists them with issues, strategy and development. Joe is the Managing Director and has three senior managers reporting to him: a Marketing Coordinator, a Production Manager and an Administration Manager. Joe has systematised the business and developed Key Performance Indicators for the company and each senior role. The team meets regularly both as a group and one-to-one with Joe to ensure that the business is on target.

Brand

The competitive basis of Primo Estate is its quality and individuality, the exclusive beauty of its packaging, its outstanding properties and its public relations expertise. One of the most important challenges facing the company has been to reinvent the Primo Estate and Joseph brands. The new cellar door and distribution centre will have a critical role in making these brands more accessible and positioning them so that they are readily distinguishable. The greatest threat is the proliferation of brands and the diminishing shelf space available in the marketplace.

For niche brands like Primo Estate and Joseph, it is essential that they become a part of potential customers' hearts and minds. Recently, the company has focused on some serious positioning work; it is now a brand that celebrates La Dolce Vita (the sweet life) Australian-style. This includes a passion for life, a sense of family, and an enjoyment of the fine art of eating. The brand essence is "the seductive elegance of Italian-style winemaking", underpinned by the brand values which are Innovative, Romantic, Italian Lifestyle and Artisan.

Strategic Issues

The most important issues facing Primo Estate include: developing the effectiveness of the brands; an oversupply of grapes industry-wide; the Australian dollar exchange rate which affects exports; consolidation of distribution channels by major retail chains; managing vineyards for sustainability, particularly with water resources; and the competitiveness of the industry.

INSIGHTS INTO
Developing a Successful Niche Business

Joe and Dina have had such great success with their niche business for a number of reasons. First and foremost is their creative approach to products and infrastructure, which is reflected through their choice of innovatively designed equipment. Their multicultural heritage has also been an important factor, as has Joe's primary aim of exploring the wonders and magic of the universe through winemaking. Then there is the major business development process implemented from 1998 – 2002 that changed the business strategy, structure and culture, arising from Joe's participation in the excellent E-Myth Mastery program.

Another factor in Primo Estate's success is the reinvention of the brand. In this case, the brand was re-examined, the fundamental underlying values were re-evaluated and restated, and a modified positioning statement and brand refreshment process was undertaken. This comprehensive process was instrumental in the refinement of their thinking and was responsible for moving them to a new position.

Joe and Dina Grilli are quite different in their approach and in their thinking, but their combined talents and enthusiasm have enabled them to develop a very successful partnership. Joe is an optimist, a "blue sky" thinker, while Dina is more of a realist and brings some of Joe's high-flying ideas back down to earth – she can see when the sky is partly cloudy! Dina has contributed enormously with her design and people skills and in developing the feel of the brand. This is most noticeable in the design of the winery at Virginia and in the new cellar door and distribution centre at McLaren Vale. Dina also provides creative input into products, labels and corporate image with a flair and sophistication that is extremely complementary to Joe's passionate winemaking focus. These skills balance Joe's approach and expertise very well indeed.

The final factor in Primo Estate's success is Joe's philosophy and approach to the business – that life is more important than business and that your business should serve your life. The essence of Primo Estate captures and epitomises the wholeness, integration and contribution of both Joe and Dina and is a reflection of their personal relationship. True love is about balance – supporting your partner and at the same time challenging them.

With such a strong brand and partnership, it's no wonder that Primo Estate is such an extraordinary company with great potential for the future.

WHAT ARE THE SECRETS OF YOUR SUCCESS AS A CEO?

I think I'm quite strong internally, but also compassionate. I think it comes over positively with my staff, as well as externally.

What does successful CEO thinking take?

Understanding the extent to which the CEO sets the culture.

What are the biggest challenges and opportunities of being a great CEO?

Challenges: I think the greatest challenge for me is to recognise my weaknesses and work on those.

Opportunities: I believe that anybody can become a great CEO; it's all in your mind. The best thing to do is to feed your mind with great thinking. I'm a huge believer in doing whatever self-improvement you can; reading books on being successful, going to seminars and having personal coaching.

What is the one thing, if it could be done, that would have the greatest impact on you as a CEO?

Any limitations that I have are within me; they are inside. So, if I could just have more wisdom and better judgment, this would have a huge impact.

What has been your biggest disappointment as a CEO?

I think that after almost 30 years in the same company, in the same business, I suppose I've seen other newer companies achieve greater heights, and I'm not talking about just sales and moneymaking, but rather reputation. So, it is lack of achievement in reputation, not just in size.

What key decisions have led to your success?

In 1998, when I decided to really get help and re-engineer the company through undertaking the E-Myth Mastery Course. What I did with that is the single biggest change.

How many hours a week do you work?

I would say 45 hours a week.

How do you plan?

I aim to plan the week on a Sunday evening and then I just have a few things that I prioritise every day.

What are the major factors in your role as a CEO that have helped you, hindered you and blocked change?

Helped you: Personal coaching and the E-Myth Mastery Course. That was a real paradigm shift.

Hindered you: Everything that hinders me is within me; just the baggage that I carry.

Blocked change: Same as what's hindered me.

What part has innovation played in your company?

We've been a huge innovator with products since day one. I'm a technician at heart, I'm a trained winemaker, and I came out of Roseworthy with a huge ambition to make innovative products.

How and when have you transitioned your role?

I am a classic technician who was thrown into a CEO role in 1986 when Dina came along. We bought out the family, and I still really continued that until 1998. Then, after doing the E-Myth Mastery course in 1998, I changed dramatically, and as a consequence, so did the company.

What is your succession plan and exit strategy?

I still feel like I'm at the beginning, so I do not have a strong sense of wanting to retire or have a successor. I'm very excited about the new beginning, the re-birth that we're going through now and I am setting up the company so that I can keep my options open. It could be anything from selling the company to handing it down in a controlled way to family members. I'm engineering the company so those options are open. In the near future, I'll structure the company to enable it to run without me, so all those options are possible.

What is business success to you?

If what you've done in business is in keeping with what your own personal aim in life is, if you've managed to get those two in alignment, I think you're being very successful. In my case, business success is to be aligned with my primary aim.

What problems do you, as a CEO, talk about on a day-to-day basis?

For us it's team issues, making sure the organisation team is happy. Making sure that all decisions are in line with the strategic objective – I'm a big believer that a lot of people get sidetracked. It is important to keep that focus, which means (learning) what to say "No" to and what to say "Yes" to.

What are the issues that you have to deal with in your leadership role as a CEO?

Being called on to represent the company in presentations of all types. Keeping my team happy.

Ensuring that all decisions are focused on the strategic objective and that we don't get sidetracked down unproductive roads.

How has individual and group mentoring helped you?

It has been critical. I've learned late in my career that mentoring and coaching is absolutely vital, and not only vital to success but also quite stimulating and enjoyable.

How do you allow the space and time for creative thinking for yourself and your staff?

It's a total mindset; really, you've got to distance yourself from a lot of the day-to-day stuff. Only the very important day-to-day stuff should get through to the CEO. Most days, probably one third to a half of the day is completely under my control and I could choose to do nothing but just think about things – that's the way I think CEOs should set it up.

What changes have you observed in the workplace culture to remain competitive to employ Generation Y?

I think the culture at Primo Estate that we've created is very much in tune with the future and younger generations because we really do have a culture of "life is more important than work". People also want to do well and achieve a lot in their job because if they're not achieving something challenging and exciting, they're not going to be happy. Our culture is all about keeping people challenged and excited.

What is your company doing to become "green"?

In our vineyards we have just minimal chemical input. Environmental and recycling and all "green" issues are permanently on the staff meeting agenda. We're in an industry where there's a lot of packaging in wine and olive oil – bottles, glass, cartons etc. – so we're a member of a national packing covenant, which really focuses on recycling and no wastage.

What impact has the business had on your life?

I'm fortunate in that I'm able to really make my primary aim in life come true. My business is a part of that so it's helping me express things that are important to me, like creativity, and it's given me freedom to choose.

If you could change one thing, what would it be?

It would be me. I know I have some big blind spots and big weaknesses, and if I could just change one of those, that's what I'd change.

Do you have to sacrifice your own life and family to be successful in business? Any comments?

Having done it both ways, I can categorically say you absolutely do not have to. You can live a café lifestyle and have a phenomenally successful business.

How have you capitalised on your business and developed it in an extraordinary way, geometrically?

I don't work that many hours and the business is running better than ever. How have I been able to do that? Just by engineering major change through the E-Myth Mastery Program. It has worked for me 120%. I have almost tripled my business in a relatively short time.

How has your development as a leader maximised your impact on all of the stakeholders you work with?

Key employees particularly – I've allowed my employees to really have the benefit of accomplishing things that I thought I had to do, so that was a paradigm shift, and that's just added to the sense of satisfaction.

How has your life developed to make you a better person and how have you maximised this?

Running a successful business allows you to help all the people with whom you come into contact to flourish. Whether they are an employee, a customer or a supplier, they go away with something more than they had before coming into contact with us.

How have you used the effects of your success to maximise your impact on the community?

Positive vibrations emanate from Primo Estate, whether you enjoy our product or you enjoy working with us, or whether you supply to us. I think all of what we've done has positive vibrations, big and small, throughout the community. It's quite satisfying.

Lessons you have Learned as a CEO

You're got to have passion. The CEO has to carry the passion of what the company is doing. Without that, the CEO and the company will both lose their way. I'm a big believer in systems doing the work and people doing the systems. So, no matter how good your people are, the company should run systemically. Hire the people to run the systems, and have a great, well documented hiring and recruiting system.

The brand is the only asset any business really has, so nurture it and look after it.

I'm a big believer in persistence and thinking long-term, not just in the next six or 12 months.

Reinvest in the future, as we did with the new cellar door – and not just the short-term future. I've always committed all the resources the company has to invest in its future. That has been something we've done from day one. I regard that as vital.

When you hire the right people, and they do a great job, make sure they get acknowledged for their contribution. I have found that recognising even the little things people do (and not just at performance reviews) improves the workplace enormously.

It is absolutely vital to have a mentor and coach – it's not only vital to success, but is also stimulating and enjoyable.

Make a commitment to re-engineer the company as I did – it caused my company to triple in size.

Be prepared to invest in your company's facility – it will pay dividends (like our new $2 million cellar door and headquarters).

Final Word

I'm a big believer in being an entrepreneur. I think the entrepreneurial spirit is such a positive spirit because it allows you to be more positive than in other role, and you have an opportunity to really contribute to the betterment of humankind. So, if I'm a good entrepreneurial role model, I'm happy with that.

Questions for Contemplation

After reading Joe's story you might like to consider:

1. What inspired you about this story?
2. What major changes do you need to make to re-engineer your business?
3. What new things do you need to create to maximise your brand?
4. What paradigm shift in your thinking do you need to make to go forward?
5. What reinvestment of time and money do you need to make?

Favorite Books

The E-Myth Revisited, by Michael E. Gerber
Enzo Ferrari, by Brock Yates

Contact Details

Joe Grilli

CEO

Primo Estate Wines

Email: jgrilli@primoestate.com.au

Website: www.primoestate.com.au

Surviving a Legal Challenge

How would you handle a serious legal challenge against you and your company?

Richard Hamood

Born: 1958

Education: Prince Alfred College, Year 12.

Career: Retail Assistant – 3 years; Family Retail Liquor Company – 18 years; Master Franchisee, Lenard's South Australia and Northern Territory – 1993-present.

Personal: Richard is a golf and motor racing fan but likes to spend most of his time with his family.

"Insist, insist, insist before going to court that all parties negotiate, even if it means locking everyone away for days on end in order to achieve a resolution because the alternative, court action, can have little reward. Our justice system does not always deliver justice to those who deserve it."

Background

Richard Hamood originally cut his teeth in business in the retail liquor and hotel industry, where he worked for over 20 years. Backed with his experience in retailing, construction, leasing and customer service, in 1993 he purchased the Lenard's Master Franchise rights for South Australia.

Within his first eight weeks as Master Franchisee he had opened four stores creating the foundation for Lenard's in South Australia. In 1999, his company acquired the Lenard's Northern Territory Master Franchise, which ultimately took the number of stores in his stable to over 30. These outlets are located in major shopping centres throughout South Australia and the Northern Territory and employ over 300 people. Each year, through these outlets, 1.6 million customers are served fresh chicken products that are taken home to be cooked and served to an estimated 6.5 million people per annum, with a combined sales value nearing $20 million. It is this success that has made Lenard's a household name in these regions.

Products and Services

Lenard's major products and services are offered through a retail franchising system that sells fresh and value-added poultry. Lenard's has been a recognised Australian leader in franchised fresh food retailing for the past 18 years. Because of outstanding innovation and customer service, the company received national retailing awards in 2002, 2003, 2005 and 2006 and in 2002, Lenard's was named National Retailer of the Year.

Established in 1987 by Master Butcher, Lenard Poulter, Lenard's has grown to more than 180 stores nationally through the application of a proven franchise system. It serves more than 11 million customers annually and generated more than $140 million in sales in the 2005/2006 financial year. From an initial range of value-added, ready-to-cook poultry meals, Lenard's has emerged as the Australian market leader to provide value-added poultry to increasingly time-challenged customers.

Growth Trends

As stated earlier, Richard Hamood established over 30 Lenard's stores in South Australia and the Northern Territory in 14 years. He remembers the biggest issue for growth in the early years was two-fold: first, finding premium sites in South Australia and Northern Territory's best shopping centres, and second, being accepted by leasing agents and landlords. However, as Lenard's and its brand awareness grew, landlords and leasing agents began to understand the value of having an emerging national brand in their centres, giving them a competitive edge, higher profile and increased security for their assets.

Market research undertaken by Lenard's has shown that today's consumers are under extreme time pressure and that the majority of Australian families have both parents working. The result is that on average, people want to spend only 20 minutes in the kitchen preparing meals and most consumers use prepared ingredients in meal preparation. Also, 80% of evening meal decisions are made on a same-day basis and 40% of meal decisions have not been made by 4.00pm. In summary, consumers are seeking quick and easy meal solutions but still want to have some involvement in preparing a meal. This is a worldwide home-cooked meal replacement trend and in Australia it is estimated to become a $1 billion industry when it matures. So Lenard's range of easy to buy, easy to cook, heat and eat products will ensure that its franchisees are well placed to take advantage of this growth market.

Income for Richard's business is generated in a number of ways: from each store's weekly sales through franchise royalties; franchise licence and construction consultancy fees each time a new store is built; franchisee training fees; assignment fees each time an existing franchisee sells their franchise; and franchise renewal fees each time an existing franchise agreement reaches the commencement of their second 10 year term.

At the individual store level as well as at the Master Franchise level, Richard believes there is significant potential for additional growth. In addition, there are a number of strategies (both actual and conceptual) to increase growth and income over the next 20 years. These include: attracting more customers to existing stores; increasing the average dollar spend by existing customers in those stores; growth of sales in the Home Meal Replacement Range; opening additional franchised stores, with new sites already identified; expansion of Lenard's inside supermarkets; entry to second tier sites and country towns; the concept of Lenard's Wholesale Food Service Franchise to provide food supplies to existing Lenard's South Australian/Northern Territory franchise outlets and the broader Food Service Industry; and the concept of mobile catering vans servicing events such as concerts, food and wine festivals, sporting and other community events.

Performance

The business has performed well owing to the proven business systems, secure weekly cash flow and Lenard's national support network. This support includes administrative systems, centralised advertising, marketing, direct product development, quality assurance systems and staff training programs.

At the store level, franchisees are supported by field staff and operational and management infrastructure systems through well-documented processes and manuals. Lenard's has also established quality assurance protocols with their suppliers. Franchisees record their store performance and document daily operations. Key Performance Indicators are tracked and trends analysed and evaluated. An electronic point of sale system with touch screen technology enables franchisees and master franchisees to take their business to new levels and to monitor performance in a number of new and effective ways.

Structure

Lenard's South Australia/Northern Territory has a dedicated team led by Richard Hamood, who, as Master Franchisee, is responsible for leasing, franchising, store development and expansion. He is supported by experienced Retail Field Managers who are jointly responsible for South Australia and the Northern Territory. The Office Administrator completes the team and is responsible for the control and daily running of the state office. Richard is backed by a team of professional managers in Lenard's national office in Brisbane, whose role is to support and develop both the franchise system and franchisees.

Brand

The Lenard's brand is widely recognised as a leader in franchising and fresh food retailing. It has proven itself to be one of Australia's most innovative business systems. It has a reputation for quality, freshness, innovation, relevance to the marketplace and excellent customer service. Underpinning this brand awareness is an extensive national marketing program that is funded by franchisees contributing 3% of their gross weekly turnover. Lenard's also supplements this through additional pooled income derived from suppliers' rebates, called the "sales pool". This sales pool was established in 2000 and has helped lift sales further in its franchise outlets.

Strategic Issues

There are many important issues facing Lenard's South Australia/Northern Territory which include finding the right franchisees and staff; compliance by franchisees to the Lenard's system; landlords increasing rents; the potential impact of bird flu; raising the overall level of franchisees' performance; rectifying issues resulting in poor performing franchises; improving profits; and the direction of Lenard's national office.

Recently, the most critical problem has been dealing with a legal challenge from a failed former franchisee, which has highlighted the importance of selecting the right franchisees through improved selection criteria. Bank managers, government employees, teachers, nurses, trades people and retailers are examples of the kinds of people who have become successful franchisees. However, the selection, training and retention of franchisees are still critical issues along with franchisees embracing change, in particular when new technology comes along.

INSIGHTS INTO

Surviving a Legal Challenge

In 2004, a former failed franchisee (a husband and wife partnership) took legal action in the Federal Court against Lenard's, Richard and his company, by claiming there had been a breach of the Trades Practices Act and that they were misled by the site selection process and sales and profit expectations. The initial judge ruled in favour of the franchisees despite extensive disclaimers in the franchise disclosure documents and despite the fact that the franchisees obtained independent legal and financial advice before signing. Richard and Lenard's were then ordered to pay substantial damages to the franchisees.

However, this ruling was successfully appealed in 2005 when the Full Federal Court unanimously overturned the decision on the basis that the franchise marketing material, contract documentation and the actions of the Master Franchisee were not misleading or open to misinterpretation by any reasonable person. The franchisees and their legal advisers subsequently and unsuccessfully appealed to the High Court of Australia.

At the heart of this case was the question of who should carry the risk of a new franchise – the master franchisor, the master franchisee or the franchisee? The original judgment could have allowed poor performing franchisees, in any franchise system, from lawn mowing to real estate, to blame anyone else but themselves for failing and therefore be able to demand financial compensation. The implications for the entire franchising industry could have been dire. Ultimately, this case demonstrated the need for franchise documentation to be simple and unambiguous, to clearly state the imperative for potential franchisees to obtain independent professional advice, and that franchising is not, and never has been, a guarantee for success.

This case went on for over four years, placing Richard Hamood in a position of having to defend his business, himself and the entire Lenard's and franchise systems. Following on from this decision, the franchisees' lot has been disastrous – they lost their franchise and their assets, and became liable for the heavy court costs and full damages. Fortunately, persistence, commitment and determination for justice were recognised by the court system. However, it cost Richard and his company an enormous amount of time, resources and energy to defend their position. Compensation, although awarded, was never received as the franchisees were declared bankrupt and their company placed into administration with no funds available to pay the compensation.

WHAT ARE THE SECRETS OF YOUR SUCCESS AS A CEO?

I never lose sight of the times when I have not been successful; these times have given me strength and experience to learn and move forward. Also, lessons from the past cement my feet firmly to the ground and keep me humble.

What does successful CEO thinking take?

Conscientiousness, honesty, making hard decisions sooner rather than later, and always challenging assumptions.

What are the biggest challenges and opportunities of being a great CEO?

Challenges: The American industrialist, Dr W. Edwards Deming, said that, "If the first 15% of a process is not right then the project will fail". I liken this to the trajectory of an arrow; if the aim is 15% out at the point of release then you are guaranteed to miss your target. If you get the first 15% right then the remaining 85% will follow, giving you a greater chance for success.

Another challenge is to know when, as a CEO, it's time to go – this should be when the hunger and passion for the business are gone. As a CEO, this is sometimes hard to accept.

Opportunities: The future. After recognising that it is time to move on, take the opportunity to free your mind and dream of the future.

What is the one thing if, it could be done, that would have the greatest impact on you as a CEO?

Being tougher earlier.

What has been your biggest disappointment as a CEO?

Experiencing the court system. I always believed that justice was one of the cornerstones of our wonderful country. I never, in my wildest dreams, imagined how easy it would be for misguided people, led by litigious-minded lawyers, to challenge a person's honesty and integrity.

What key decisions have led to your success?

Not letting the detail get in the way of the vision.

How many hours a week do you work?

About 70 to 80 hours a week before we had our first child, but that has now reduced because I don't want to leave my wife and new born son in the morning and I can't wait to get back to see them in the evening.

How do you plan?

Sometimes with structure, sometimes on the go, but planning is not always my strength.

What are the major factors in your role as a CEO that have helped you, hindered you and blocked change?

Helped you: Networking with the TEC group; my wife's support and my family's faith in me.

Hindered you: Under-performing franchisees and direction from the National Office.

Blocked change: Franchisees' reluctance to implement change.

What part has innovation played in your company?

Little, as the mechanics of our business today are not dissimilar to what they were 14 years ago.

How and when have you transitioned your role?

I've moved away from being at stores and in stores and have taken on a much more administrative role, simply due to the direction of the industry. We're more like a legal firm in some respects than a franchising firm these days in how we do business. A large part of what we do is covering our back against potential legal action.

What is your succession plan?

To prepare the business to a point that if the proverbial bus comes around the corner, a sale process is all documented and able to be easily followed by others.

What is your exit strategy?

Preparing the business for sale by the use of external organisations, incorporating a sales and marketing campaign. Also making sure that our business is presented in an orderly and effective way so that someone doing due diligence will be able to easily assess their potential purchase.

What is business success to you?

Making the Lenard's brand a household name in South Australia and the Northern Territory.

What problems do you, as a CEO, talk about on a day-to-day basis?

The overall direction of the business and our franchisees' weekly performance and growth.

What are the issues that you have to deal with in your leadership role as a CEO?

The unrealistic expectations of some franchisees who expect someone else, not them, will make their business successful.

How has individual and group mentoring helped you?

I'm as not impetuous as I once was; I think about things much more. It has helped me to move forward in many areas. It has made me a wiser person, but boy, have I made some mistakes along the way.

What changes have you observed in the workplace culture to remain competitive to employ Generation Y?

We are finding it difficult to satisfy employees from Generation Y as our industry is based around good, old-fashioned, hard, physical, hands-on-work. Generation Y has moved away from the hands-on culture and are more at home with computers and the mind work that goes with them.

What impact has the business had on your life?

My life has been influenced by the people I have met and the books I have read. I have learnt never to make assumptions about a person and I am constantly surprised when I learn about their life and their achievements.

Richard Hamood

Do you have to sacrifice your own life and family to be successful in business? Any comments?

For me, yes, because two of the components to achieve success are pure hard work and long hours. If you have a very large company and top performing managers then you could run things differently. But, historically, I've been a long hours person. It's become habitual, but it's a habit that I'd like to change when I've developed a business that doesn't require me as much.

How have you capitalised on your business and developed it in an extraordinary way, geometrically?

Not yet. Sometimes, through no fault of your own, you find that your industry has taken you down a different pathway from the one you had planned.

How has your development as a leader maximised your impact on all of the stakeholders you work with?

I've been honest, so I show honesty. Also, I show stability, along with compassion for people and their families. This has developed a culture where we don't shoot from the hip – we think about what we do before we do it.

How has your life developed to make you a better person and how have you maximised this?

I'm more knowledgeable than I would have been. I'm more analytical than I would have been and I'm more appreciative of my wife, family and people that surround me, than I would have been. Having a wonderful wife and beautiful children bring out dormant qualities that drive you to succeed. I only wish I had understood this at an earlier age!

Lessons you have Learned as a CEO

Numbers never lie.

Be decisive.

Learn to accept failure; learn from it and move forward.

Survive and do whatever it takes.

Your goal must always be success, irrespective of circumstances.

Mix with and learn from good people.

Never assume and always do your homework.

Know when it's time to move on.

Don't assume that other people know or understand your business.

Toughness. If I had a choice, I'd choose to be more successful over being better liked – the best leaders are not always the best liked and being more successful yourself creates more success for other people who surround you.

Don't assume the legal system knows your industry.

Court cases can suck you dry of time, money, energy and creativity.

Never underestimate the old boys club in the legal industry, which could work against you.

The longer a court case goes, the further away it is from the actual core issues that started the case in the first place. It becomes embroiled in legal argument that has little relevance to the dispute.

Always be ready to sell your business.

Continue to further your education and be mentored through a peer group like TEC.

Richard Hamood

Honesty; a strong work ethic; leaving a financial and moral inheritance that will give a strong base for future generations.

Questions for Contemplation

As you reflect on Richard's life, ask yourself:

1. If you could mix with better people sooner and make tougher decisions earlier, would you? If the answer is obvious, then do it.

2. How tough are you in addressing issues? What do you need to change and take action on?

3. Where are you at? Do you need to exit what you are doing and find your next challenge or chase your next goal or dream?

4. What is important to you? How are you manifesting it?

Favorite Book

How to Win Friends and Influence People, by Dale Carnegie
The Richest Man in Babylon, by George Clason

Contact Details

Richard Hamood

Managing Director

Poulet Frais Pty Ltd

Email: richardh@lenardssant.com.au

Website: www.lenards.com.au

Passing On the Baton in a Family Business

How would you position your company to be a leader in an industry of copycats and look-a-likes?

Anthony Toop
& Karen Raffen

Anthony Toop

Born: 1957

Education: Year 12, Prince Alfred College; three years of B. Business (Property Resource Management), South Australia Institute of Technology; Real Estate Certificate; Restricted Builder's Licence.

Career: Toop's Electrical, Peterborough, 1974-76; Real Estate Sales 1976-85; Toop & Toop 1986-present.

Personal: Vineyards, farming, wine, travel, Harley Davidsons and go-karting.

Karen Raffen

Born: 1970

Education: Year 12, Heathfield High School; B. Business (Human Resource and Marketing Management), University of South Australia; Associate Diploma Business, South Australia Institute of Technology; Real Estate Certificate in Sales.

Career: Range of positions including HR Assistant, Marketing Coordinator/Sales Representative, Sales and Marketing Manager, and National Sales and Marketing Manager, Chief Kitchenware, 1992-2000; Industry Development Manager, Department of Industry and Trade, 2001; Marketing Manager, San Remo, 2001; range of positions including Assistant General Manager and General Manager, Toop and Toop, 2001-present. Appointed CEO January 2006.

Personal: Snow skiing, walking, running, rollerblading, mountain bike riding, cooking and reading novels.

"If it were not for our passion to be the best and drive change, we would not have achieved the success that we have. It's what pushes you through the pain barrier."

Anthony Toop—Managing Director

"You only get out of something what you put into it. Things just don't fall into your lap; you have to make them happen."

Karen Raffen—CEO

Background

In 1985, after working in the real estate industry for 10 years, Anthony and Sylvia Toop sold an investment property and used the $20,000 proceeds to establish Toop & Toop from their home.

Products

Toop & Toop specialises in residential real estate and property management. It is the largest independent agency in Adelaide and has the highest brand profile in this category. It is the only company of its size not to deal with commercial property.

Growth Trends

Several factors contributed to Toop & Toop's success including: opening two new offices; buying new rent rolls; doubling the business through acquisitions; restructuring the management of the company including appointing a General Manager and a Financial Manager; and the use of technology and innovation. Currently the company has four offices which are 100% company owned and managed. These offices handle annual property sales in excess of $600 Million.

Performance

Toop & Toop has performed against a backdrop of: economic downturn; government regulation; large international businesses moving into the industry; high competition; low barriers to entry; poor quality; over supply of agents; and public perception of agents.

The company has expanded and dominated its market sector despite emerging local and international brands, margin squeeze and consolidation of competitors. This is thanks to a great team, strong brand and culture, quality systems and products, and passionate leadership.

Toop & Toop has achieved extraordinary results. It is one of the most highly awarded residential real estate companies in Australia. Awards include:

- The Telstra/SA Government Small Business Award in 1997
- Five State and National Awards from the Australian Customer Service Association, including the National Award for 2004
- Australia Day Council Business Award 2000
- Induction into the Family Business of Australia Hall of Fame 2005
- REISA 2005 Awards for Website of the Year, Corporate Marketer of the Year, Medium Agency

of the Year, Large Agency of the Year, Overall Agency of the Year and Team Sales Person of the Year

- REIA 2005 Award for Innovation and Communication
- Australian Business Excellence Awards, SME Award 2006
- First residential real estate company to achieve ISO9002 Quality Accreditation
- REISA 2006 Awards for Website of the Year, Corporate Marketing Campaign of the Year, Innovation of the Year, Top Salesperson of the Year, Agency of the Year (Large), Property Management Agency of the Year (Large), Local Residential Salesperson of the Year (East/City) and Local Salesperson of the Year (Hills).
- REIA 2007 National Awards for Best Innovation, Residential Sales Person of the Year and Large Agency of the Year.

Toop & Toop pioneered the application of technology to real estate which include: a selling system called Virtual Agent; virtual inspections; Internet and SMS-based marketing systems and secure inspections. It also produces a weekly property publication, colour press advertisements, initiation of loan furniture, consulting on professional presentation, floodlit and pictorial display boards and auction price guidelines.

The company is well poised to expand locally and nationally because it can move quickly and is not locked into a large, slow moving, international franchise organisation.

Structure

The company has a Board (comprising the CEO, external accountant and Sylvia and Anthony Toop). The CEO has a management team comprising five senior managers including a Property Manager, a Finance Manager, an Advertising Studio Manager, a Human Resources Manager and an Administration Manager. The CEO also covers a Sales Manager role. The company has just under 100 staff including 35 sales agents. There are no branch managers; the organisational structure is very flat.

Brand

Toop & Toop's unique marketing, advanced technology, reputation, ethics and service are the backbone of its brand. Through these attributes, Toop & Toop appears to be positioned as the strongest independent real estate brand in South Australia. Brand development has been aided by the owners' high profile and involvement with the community.

Strategic Issues

The most important issues facing the business include an increasingly competitive, uncertain environment, and ensuring the business has good people and clear strategic direction. The implementation of a sophisticated Customer Relationship Management process and high-level internal sales training will ensure ongoing outcomes at a high level.

INSIGHTS INTO

Passing on the Baton in a Family Business

There is always a challenge in any business or company where there is a succession process for a leader. This is particularly true with a family business and where the founder still remains in the business part-time. It is inevitable that there will be a blurring and overlapping of roles, and some tension between the owner and the new CEO. What follows is a summary of the secrets of successfully passing on the baton in a family business.

First of all, have a good reason to appoint a CEO. In Anthony's case, Karen had been General Manager for five years and had already proven herself. Anthony had made a conscious decision to step away from the day-to-day running of the agency to develop several new business interests and to take on an ambassadorial role for Toop & Toop. It's simple to choose the right time to make the transition by remembering that the time is *always* right because *there is no right time*.

Then there is a need to have clear expectations and agreements in place with the new CEO for their role and performance – and it is imperative that owners establish and communicate a clear direction for their business. If the owner doesn't know what he wants, how can his successor possibly know? However, neither owners nor replacement CEOs should have too many performance expectations during the transition period. It's important that a new CEO understudies the owner over a period of time to ensure that they are clear on "how we do things around here" and so that they do not misguidedly try to change the company culture overnight.

Any issues or disagreements arising should ideally be managed with the help of an external mentor who is trusted by both the owner and the new CEO. A professional, unbiased and external perspective eases tension and assists in developing solutions.

In addition to these critical factors, there are a number of other points to remember for a smooth transition between owner and new CEO. The owner may consciously or unconsciously be unable or unwilling to give up their space and role in the business, even though they may only be part-time and initially wanted to step back. Naturally, old habits and patterns die hard, so one solution is for the owner to take extended leave, go overseas and stay well away from the business for at least three months, allowing the new incumbent time and breathing space to settle in.

It can be very helpful for the owner to be mentored in the process of letting go, which can be a difficult and traumatic undertaking – people often see the business (over which they shed plenty of blood, sweat and tears) as their "baby". It is understandable then, that they may experience some loss of identity, a loss of control and be concerned about what their new role is, both at work and in the community.

Negotiate a clear understanding with regard to the owner being absent from the business and then returning to the business. This can create a dilemma if the owner feels a loss of control, fear and concern that the business has been performing *without* them. There is also the worry about whether the business is going in the "right" direction, whatever that is. It is suggested that the owner clearly articulates their performance expectations for the business and holds the CEO accountable for them. The owner should identify the parts of the business they really enjoy and then create a role around these, leaving the CEO to manage everything else. The new CEO should hold regular update sessions for the owner to keep them briefed on progress and performance.

The best way to handle these issues is for the owner to recognise them and give the new CEO space to perform – after all, it's their job now. Owners must be careful to let the new CEO make their own mark in due course and must not deliberately or unconsciously interfere.

Lastly, appoint a Board with external Directors, one of whom becomes Chairman. This will allow an ongoing, objective forum for the new CEO to access support and assist the owner to change to the new.

In the instance of Anthony Toop and Karen Raffen, navigating this tricky transition happened because of mutual respect, understanding, patience and solid mentoring. As Karen says, "I can still draw wisdom from him and bounce ideas off him. If you see a relay in the Olympics, when they pass the baton, some pass it quickly and some pass it slower, but more securely. I believe the baton has been passed in a very considered way".

WHAT ARE THE SECRETS OF YOUR SUCCESS AS A CEO?

A.T.   Recognising and accepting my weaknesses, and plugging them with experts; joining a CEO peer group; thinking independently; knowing the business well; trusting my instincts and being prepared to back them and take the consequences.

K.R.   Being able to read situations quickly then act appropriately to get the outcome I need; bringing together external and internal influences to meet strategic objectives; having a clear vision and the passion to achieve it.

What are the biggest challenges and opportunities of being a great CEO?

A.T. — The greatest challenge was to get out of the detail into a more strategic role, and resist the temptation to go back to where it's comfortable.

K.R. — If it is a family business, the greatest challenge is dealing with the owners. If it is a big business, it's dealing with the Board.

What is the one thing, if it could be done, that would have the greatest impact on you as a CEO?

A.T. — If my two children joined the business.

K.R. — Having the owners give me a clear direction of where they want the business to go.

What has been your biggest disappointment as a CEO?

A.T. — That we didn't step up at the time we launched our virtual agent technology. We could have taken the world by storm but we didn't.

K.R. — I get annoyed with myself when I question my ability in this role; I'm constantly trying to make everybody happy.

How do you handle rejection and failure?

A.T. — I still have sleepless nights, which means I don't handle it that well.

K.R. — I'm really tough on myself but at the end of the day, I learn from it and move forward.

How many hours a week do you work?

A.T. — About 80 in total, but at least half are non-Toop related. It's self-inflicted.

K.R. — 55-70 hours if you include networking and social events, depending on the week.

How do you plan?

A.T. — I plan mentally, with mental pictures.

K.R. — Each morning I do a mud map of what needs to be done that day. I do more strategic planning once a month when I'm thinking about my Board report or my management report. Annually, our Board holds a strategic planning session.

What are the major factors in your role as a CEO that have helped you, hindered you and blocked change?

A.T. — *Helped you:* The support I received from my CEO mentoring group and my mentor.

— *Hindered you:* Not resolving the financial role in the business early enough.

— *Blocked change:* The never-ending fear of losing your top people, and the consequences that flow from a stable team.

K.R. — *Helped you:* The power to make certain things happen, and a great management team.

— *Hindered you:* Not moving to the next level as a CEO.

— *Blocked change:* Lack of direction from the Board.

What is your succession plan?

K.R. — To make sure I've got someone who can take over my role, but that is a long-term process.

What is your exit strategy?

A.T. — It depends on the mood of my children, but they're a decade away from being of value to the business, and a lot can happen in a decade.

What is business success to you?

A.T. — Success is feeling good about the business, what we're doing in the community and about what we're returning to the community.

K.R. — I think there are four things: the bottom line; a strong brand; customer acceptance; and high staff morale.

What problems do you, as a CEO, talk about on a day-to-day basis?

A.T. — Market share, competitor activity and margin.

K.R. — Operations, human resources, finance and strategy.

What are the issues that you have to deal with in your leadership role as a CEO?

A.T. — Reconciling passion with professionalism

is by far the biggest issue I've got.

K.R. — How you present yourself to your staff and to your clients; how you are acting as a leader and relating to the Board and owners.

How do you allow the space and time for creative thinking for yourself and your staff?

A.T. — I took up transcendental meditation. I've always taken a lot of holidays and have been very disciplined about having no business contact during those breaks.

K.R. — Exercise is my "me time" when I have time to let my subconscious work for me.

How has individual and group mentoring helped you?

A.T. — It's been fundamental. I could not have achieved the outcomes that we've got without it.

K.R. — It has helped me enormously by giving me ideas, and helping me gain confidence and develop as a person and a CEO.

What changes have you observed in the workplace culture to remain competitive to employ Generation Y?

K.R. — Career-pathing is really important. They also don't just want to come to work, do their jobs and go home. They want to have an experience and be involved in the business, its events and social functions.

What impact has the business had on your life?

K.R. — It's forced me to be much more in the public eye.

Do you have to sacrifice your own life and family to be successful in business? Any comments?

K.R. — To a certain extent, yes. I don't spend as much time with family and friends as I'd like to.

How has your life developed to make you a better person and how have you maximised this?

A.T. — I think having more time to reflect. Having

people die all around me and going to their funerals has refocused how important time is.

K.R. — Through a challenging role in a traditionally male management industry; having a wonderful husband who supports me and gives me space; and a circle of close friends and family. This allows me to take on new challenges in my career and to grow and develop.

How have you capitalised on your business and developed in an extraordinary way, geometrically?

A.T. — I've now got the business working for me, rather than me for it. It is not now controlling my entire life.

How have you developed as a leader that has maximised your impact on all the stakeholders you work with?

A.T. — I've always led from the front. There's nothing I've asked anyone to do that I wouldn't do myself.

How have you used the effects of the above three areas to maximise your impact on the community?

A.T. — The profile and the credibility that's been developed by the business are being used by charities every other week; and it's being leveraged.

Anthony Toop & Karen Raffen

Lessons you have Learned as a CEO

Anthony Toop

You need self-belief to try out new ideas; the passion to persist; and the flexibility to know when to let go.

Build a strong culture based on commitment, performance, work ethic and the high expectations of staff and clients.

A business model based on technology will create a shorter sales cycle, quicker results for clients, greater rewards for staff and lower costs for the business.

The customer is everything; focus on outstanding customer service.

Strong profits and a healthy balance sheet support investment in growth based on innovation and technology in a cyclic industry.

You can become a global leader in your industry by continually investing in and implementing innovation and research.

Establish, retain and continually grow your market leadership position to attract staff, clients and enhance your reputation and brand.

Translate your vision into a plan and series of actions.

Never implement technology for its own sake. Only do it to improve client service, differentiate you in the market place and improve efficiency.

Attract, select and retain the very best people possible and ensure that they fit the culture.

Keep travelling to develop personally and to pick up new ideas, new technology and world best practices.

Work from your own vision, which is developed through intuition. Share your ideas with a mentor or mentoring group.

Lessons you have Learned as a CEO

Karen Raffen

Keep thinking about your edge and how you keep your business fresh, alive and relevant to customers.

Manage your Board and owners. If you fail to build close relationships, trust or manage upward effectively, it is likely they will lose confidence in you.

Have a clear vision and a clear path to achieve it.

Understand your competitors and what's happening in the external environment.

Read situations quickly and adapt accordingly to get the outcomes you need.

Be committed to providing an environment that people want to work in.

Focus on the numbers.

Remember you are in a leadership role and that's how others see you.

Spend time with key staff, give them guidance, respect their openness and be open yourself. This will flow on to other staff and through them to clients.

Be strategic about managing people and introducing change into the business.

You need a well-developed strategic plan to know where you're heading.

When you accept the leadership baton as a new CEO, set clear boundaries and processes, and clarify expectations. Step up as the leader and give feedback when necessary.

Final Word

The most important thing to have is passion. Be passionate about your own life. Be passionate about your family. Be passionate about your company. Be passionate about your industry. Be passionate about your country. — ANTHONY TOOP

You are probably the only thing holding you back from greatness. You can pretty well do what you want. You just have to get out there and do it. — KAREN RAFFEN

Questions for Contemplation

As you reflect on Anthony's life ask yourself:

1. How long would you be prepared to leave your business in the hands of your team without contact?

2. How would you cope if half of your team set up across the road?

As you reflect on Karen's life ask yourself:

1. Have you actually thought through where you are personally heading and where you want to be?

2. How happy are you? If you are not very happy, what aspects of your life do you need to change because of the impact on every other part of your life?

Favorite Books

The Power of Now, by Eckhart Tolle
The 22 Immutable Laws of Marketing, by Al Ries and Jack Trout

Contact Details

Anthony Toop - Managing Director

Karen Raffen - CEO

Toop & Toop Real Estate

Email: anthony.toop@toop.com.au, karen.raffen@toop.com.au

Website: www.toop.com.au

Opera

4. Operating a National and/ or Global Business

Developing a Vertically Integrated Company

If you were in a declining industry and a global market, what would you do to survive and grow your business?

Doug Brown

Born: 1953

Education: Scott's College Primary School, Warwick, Queensland (during which period his family lived in New Guinea); Years 8-11, Findon High School, Adelaide; Year 12, Croydon High School, Adelaide; Diploma of Teaching (Secondary), Western Teachers' College, Adelaide; Graduate Diploma Computer Education, University of South Australia – Doug received a first-year pass but then withdrew to start Entech Electronics.

Career: Secondary Teacher, South Australian Education Department, 1972-74 and 1981-86; Secondary Teacher, Commonwealth Education Service, Northern Territory, 1975-80; Director, Toldale Pty Ltd, 1987; Managing Director, Entech Printed Circuits (owned by Toldale Pty Ltd); Group Managing Director, Entech Group of Companies, 1989-present.

Personal: Doug enjoys spending time with his family, reading, fishing and boating. He loves photography and is interested in computers and radio-controlled helicopters.

"Be fast and flexible and prepared to make a mistake, but do not be prepared to make a mistake you can't afford."

Background

Doug Brown started his professional life as a technical studies teacher. In 1986, after studying computing and electronics, he won a Commonwealth grant to commercialise the electronics that he was working on in education. He put together a team of four partners to complete the product. This company then bought another small company that was supplying peripheral computer products and memory board information systems applications.

The group then diversified and bought a computer software and retail outlet (Computer Programs, Machines and Services) which one partner elected to run by himself. The remaining three partners built up the circuit board side of the business and started joint ventures with other people. In time, and despite a loss of sales from the aftermath of the 9/11 terrorist attacks, the company continued to grow to reach a turnover of $45 million in 2006.

Through an extensive framework of local facilities and offshore partnerships, Entech can manufacture in the world's most competitive environments. Their local product divisions have been vertically integrated and this has allowed global procurement of products and components as an extra layer of integration, without significant risk to the group's infrastructure or focus.

In support of this strategy, their China office has been built up in both area and personnel. A key component that has built their competitive advantage is the "one stop shop" focus. In offering the customer a full range of services, be it a component, engineering services, sub-assembly or full turnkey manufacturing, they have greatly reduced the costs of sales and marketing as the customers are mostly common to all product groups.

This approach gives Entech the capacity and ability to target markets and customers of any size anywhere throughout the world, but with the primary focus on the Pacific Rim.

Products and Services

The company focuses on the design, engineering and manufacture of electronic products, and provides procurement services for components, raw materials and manufactured goods. These include: electronic manufacturing services; electronic assemblies; printed circuit products; graphics electronics products; wire harnesses, liquid crystal displays and metal enclosures.

Growth Trends

From inception, the company has grown at the rate of 10-15% per year. Since 2004, after the implementation of their China strategy to manufacture long-run, large-scale manufacturing offshore, the company has grown from $24 million in sales to $45 million in sales. Entech now boasts six sites; three in Adelaide, one in China, one in New Zealand, and one in the USA, having grown to over 200 personnel.

Growth has been achieved through intense customer focus, innovative technical skills and providing products and services that consistently have exceeded the quality and value offered by their competitors. Entech has sought to build business relationships with customers of small to medium companies (SMEs), or divisions of companies that manufacture electronic products for export. These companies have professionally and technically trained purchasing staff who buy according to specifications and accepted international standards. By necessity then, Entech develops highly technical sales relationships with their customers, and includes bilateral education in their technical service agreements to meet these needs. As a result, the company has grown significantly.

Performance

Entech's performance is based upon a well-articulated set of values that are integrated into their culture. These include a strong customer focus through the development of intense and solid long-term relationships; participation with equity so that all stakeholders receive meaningful benefit from the relationship; and honesty and trust – two key values that are both expected and given.

The company is success-oriented with successful long-term outcomes developed through technical and organisational superiority and innovation. Because of the Entech Group's complementary divisions and vertical integration, they are able to parallel process products across the company in project terms, unlike any of their competitors in the Australia/New Zealand region. Therefore, they are a faster and more efficient supplier of products and services, and as such, do not have any direct competitors in the usual sense. Their competitors see the Entech Group as a service, quality and price leader. However, Entech has great opportunities to improve, as this quality and price leadership is a consequence of the group's structural efficiency, rather than merely being a consequence of a competent, total-quality focused, lean operation.

Now that the group's integration is complete, they can offer leading-edge technologies across the company with greater affordability and efficiency. This gives the divisions the appearance of being "larger than life" when tendering and quoting on jobs and increases client confidence.

Entech's strategy of short- to medium-term, fast-turnaround products being manufactured in Australia and their slower, long-run, large-scale products being manufactured offshore has served them well.

Structure

Six shareholders own the company. The three original shareholders hold the majority of shares. They have a very functional Board comprising the six shareholders, with one of the larger shareholders acting as Chairman. Doug Brown is the Chief Executive Officer and has six senior managers reporting to him including the

New Zealand Manager, the China Manager, the Engineering Manager, the Corporate Services Manager, the Operations Manager – Printed Circuit Board, and the Operations Manager – Electronic Assembly. Business development is handled by the CEO and an assistant. Each division has their own product-focused sales teams.

Brand

The Entech Group's brand has developed quite strongly. Now, with the integration of the separate companies into one business, the focus is on Entech Electronics. The Entech Group is still the corporate vehicle but the name Entech Electronics is used to advertise what the company does; offering technical skills and services to either manufacture or assist clients to manufacture products in the best, most cost-effective way.

Strategic Issues

The most important issues facing the Entech Group are: a decreasing market in Australia for the long-run work; maintaining the capital investment in multiple capital-intensive businesses within the group; getting a better return for cost involved with a client; keeping up-to-date with technology; and developing the leadership capacity to take the company into the future.

INSIGHTS INTO

Developing a Vertically Integrated Company

Entech Electronics recently combined the operations of Entech Circuits and Graphics, and Entech Electronic Manufacturing into a single trading entity, thereby streamlining the management and delivery of a wide range of high technology engineering products and services. Entech Electronics is structured to deliver a diverse range of value-added services to their clients. With three Australian and three offshore locations, the Entech Group provides customers with highly professional local engineering staff, global expertise and access to the world's best practice suppliers. This allows the company to tailor the most appropriate solutions to a client's prototyping, product development procurement, assembly and logistics management requirements.

The company can provide a complete range of services – design, procurement, construction and supply. It can sell circuit boards to a client which has its own assembly line, sell assembly services to clients who obtain circuit boards from elsewhere, or it can do the graphics work for a circuit board that is assembled elsewhere. Alternatively, it can do the lot in-house. In addition, Entech can do fast-run prototypes required at short notice and meet high-volume long-run manufacturing needs offshore.

Thus Entech is a vertically integrated "one stop shop" that is totally flexible to meet client needs. The genius of this model is that it could be franchised elsewhere using the proven processes and strategies developed over the years. The company has a significant engineering capability to be able to design, make, test and inspect offshore. However, the company never ships directly from offshore because it cannot control the quality of products that are technically very complex. Theft of intellectual property is also a possible issue. So, only sub-parts are manufactured offshore and brought back to Australia for testing and assembly to ensure integrity, concept security and high quality. With labour costs being so high in Australia, the local facility becomes the initiating facility to do long-runs in China. China also offers the flexibility of having additional staff who can provide resources for overnight work from Australia.

Entech has the buying power as well as the complete solution in one company. The benefit this offers is that work can be done in-house using parallel processes that can facilitate meeting deadlines and reducing costs for clients and this is the reason for its great success.

Doug Brown

WHAT ARE THE SECRETS OF YOUR SUCCESS AS A CEO?

I think people management. I'm not particularly clever at anything. One of the things that I do well is looking after my people. I enjoy helping people and I do it because it is right and you get all the positives that you want.

What does successful CEO thinking take?

An endless enthusiasm to be better. Not looking for blame, but looking for answers. A willingness to share. If you are generally looking after your staff's best interests, it's a breeze.

What are the biggest challenges and opportunities of being a great CEO?

Challenges: Having to sack the major shareholder in the second year of operation and take his position and then taking the company forward.

Opportunities: To grow the company to reach its potential.

What is the one thing, if it could be done, that would have the greatest impact on you as a CEO?

It's not money; it's finding my successor. If we found a super person to be my Chief Operating Officer/CEO, it would have a tremendous impact by allowing me to get on with the more strategic, creative things to maximise the potential of this business.

What has been your biggest disappointment as a CEO?

My father's death the year I started the company. He doesn't have any knowledge of me in the company. He's not seen me as anything other than a school teacher. Yet he was a director of a multinational himself.

How do you handle rejection and failure?

As badly as the next person, if not worse. I take things to heart because I am genuinely trying to do the right thing all the time. But I bounce back and come at it. I take it as a challenge, generally.

What key decisions have led to your success?

I've taken the hard decisions whenever they have been needed. I face problems and I don't try to find excuses – I am responsible. I confront the issues as soon as they are obvious and I don't procrastinate.

How many hours a week do you work?

A lot less than I used to. I get here before 8.00am and I go at about 5.30pm. And I don't do any work on the weekends. Probably 50 hours, and most of it is thinking stuff now. My wife sees me sitting on the chair staring into the distance and she says the cogs are moving. My job is thinking; it's not putting pen to paper anymore.

How do you plan?

It's my method of operation. I go hunting for the issues and I go hunting for the solutions. Then I call all the principal people into the room and play the devil's advocate to make them justify and argue the solution because, quite often, what was reality yesterday is not reality today.

What are the major factors in your role as a CEO that have helped you, hindered you and blocked change?

Helped you: My doggedness. When I put my teeth into a task, I don't stop until it's finished.

Hindered you: My professional qualifications aren't aligned sufficiently with where I would like to be. It's too late now to be aligned with accounting and/or electronic engineering.

Blocked change: I don't think anything has blocked change to be honest. I don't think change is an issue in my life. It's not something I am fearful of and, to be honest, I quite enjoy it – it's renewing.

What part has innovation played in your company?

Everything. My whole company is about technological innovation. I get a buzz out of it.

How and when have you transitioned your role?

I am currently doing that very much at this moment. I have put into place various strategies aimed at establishing a succession path for myself within the company.

What is your succession plan?

Hiring the right COO/CEO.

What is your exit strategy?

We have two exit strategies. One is to set the business up for sale – that's the primary strategy. And the second strategy is to make it a long-term commitment, so if a sale doesn't come along on our terms, we will operate forever.

What is business success to you?

To be able to go away from the business and not have concerns of how it is operating and still remain proud of what it is doing.

What problems do you, as a CEO, talk about on a day-to-day basis?

Trying to get people to recognise their shortcomings and the issues that need to be addressed, without offending them. We've all got our shortcomings and that's what wives can do; they can tell husbands things they need to hear. This company is like a family and spouse in many respects. One of the values of a spouse is that when you get too proud, they bring you back to balance. If you are down they bring you back up. And in many ways, I see that in the company – having that balance and equanimity.

What are the issues that you have to deal with in your leadership role as a CEO?

Probably in the sales role, because I'm a very honest person and sometimes you have to sell yourself at a level that I'm not all that comfortable with. I feel it's a little dishonest sometimes and that's not me naturally. I also feel that you see so many people that you can't give them the attention and detail that you would like.

How do you allow the space and time for creative thinking for yourself and your staff?

I am a person who doesn't put pen to paper unnecessarily. I don't want people to report to me in writing; I want them to do it verbally. I can get a lot more background on a person and a creative situation by establishing the footprint face-to-face and not having to read between the lines, because you get all the body language with it. You have to put a half a day into a memo to get what you can get in 15 minutes out of a conversation! I am a good delegator. I do what I want to do because I think it is important. I don't get bogged down in paperwork or the drudgery. I allow time for creative thinking because I get a buzz out of it.

How has individual and group mentoring helped you?

It enabled me to benchmark myself against my peers and understand my performance against their performance. It challenged me to grow and to change.

What changes have you observed in the workplace culture to remain competitive to employ Generation Y?

Not a great deal. However, I think our environment is conducive to them. I think there are a lot of interesting things going on – my staff are not doing mundane things. We have a lot of clever and interesting people, so employees are happy to stay.

What impact has the business had on your life?

It has taken control of my life from time to time, but in these later years it's given me a lot of self-satisfaction and I measure myself by it.

Do you have to sacrifice your own life and family to be successful in business? Any comments?

No. I think I am being me. My wife will tell you I was worse to live with when I was a teacher. I was working seven days a week and that was hard. But you've got no choice, that's what happens. If you want to be an Olympian, you have to have an out-of-balance life to bring it into balance long-term. And you've got to have people around you who are prepared to do the same.

How have you capitalised on your business and developed it in an extraordinary way, geometrically?

There are so many little things; there are no big things. It's all the little things that keep leading it in the right direction. You roll the wheel a little bit more and you tap the front of the ship to keep it on course – it's a thousand little things. It's a constant focus on the detail because, before you know it, the whole mentality and ethic of your people could change without you noticing it.

How has your development as a leader maximised your impact on all of the stakeholders you work with?

Obviously, taking responsibility. I would saw my leg off before not keeping the commitments I make – I set the example. I don't suffer from delusions; Entech is a $45 million business. Big deal. There are millions of them out there. This has been my life and it's been the focus of my life. I don't think it is anything spectacular. I am proud of it, but there are a lot more successful businesses than this.

How has your life developed to make you a better person and how have you maximised this?

When you start taking responsibility and there is nobody standing behind you to pass the buck to, you start to understand that you don't have any option but to succeed. You start developing a level of maturity and see that you don't have to win every battle, but you are not allowed to lose the ones that will kill you. So, you fight battles you can win or can afford to lose. It's having good judgement; being discerning. If you take a lot of little steps, and it starts to go in the wrong direction, you can quickly make a change.

Lessons you have Learned as a CEO

Don't scare your employees out of honesty.

Don't dominate them.

Don't encourage failure, but be accepting of it if it's happened despite the best of intentions based on solid fact.

Value people so they know it.

Don't lose sight of your targets.

Don't compromise your standards or your values, and don't confuse those with pride or greed.

Get good people around you and develop them so you can depend on them and them on you.

Manage with honesty. I translate that a little bit further and say in every negotiation I have with my staff that if it's 50/50, it goes their way, not mine. I'm with people who don't feel like they are going to be taken advantage of.

Take responsibility in business. When necessary, be bold and courageous, taking a stand for what is true and right – for example, my sacking a major shareholder/Managing Director.

Step up when necessary and have a go. Get in the game of the CEO and play it happily with 49%. Then I'm happy to give 51% of what we do.

Be generous.

Don't hassle over the small stuff.

How much is enough? You want to keep going and it's so much easier to work with persistence, determination and flair.

Always be willing to change and learn.

Doug Brown

Final Word

Final Word

It's the old cliché of being true to yourself. If you can't live with what you are doing, don't do it. If you don't like the heat in the kitchen, get out. If you don't believe in what you are doing, don't do it. If the pressure is going to kill you, you are in the wrong game. If you don't want to get up and go to work, then go and do something else – you've picked the wrong job.

Questions for Contemplation

As you reflect on Doug's life, ask yourself:

1. How much are you enjoying life?
2. How true are you being to yourself?
3. What excuses are you making for doing what you are doing?
4. How much are your activities aligned with your primary aim?

Favorite Book

The Rise and Rise of Kerry Packer, by Paul Barry
Too Long in the Bush, by Len Beadell

Contact Details

Doug Brown

Managing Director

Entech Electronics

Email: djbrown@entechgroup.net

Website: www.entechgroup.net

Growing a Company by Developing a Fantastic Culture

What would you do to run a profitable business with one large government customer?

Kim Scott

Born: 1965

Education: Year 12, Westminster College; Bachelor of Engineering (Mechanical Engineering), First Class Honours, University of Adelaide, 1986.

Career: Started at Defence Science and Technology Organisation (DSTO) in Guided Weapons Division in 1987, working two years at US Army Missile Command in Huntsville, Alabama; joined C.J. Abell and Co in 1992 as Systems Engineer, rising through project and business management; led the Electronic Warfare (EW) and Command, Control, Communications and Intelligence (C4I) lines of business for Tenix when it acquired Vision Abell Pty Ltd in 2000; appointed General Manager, Electronic Systems Division, 2003.

Personal: Father of two children, Caed and Ashlee, with wife Megan, enjoys cycling, modern literature, playing bass guitar, restoring and modifying cars.

"It's often talked about – always open yourself up to new learning. Never believe you will stop learning. You will stop learning the day you die. I think if you keep yourself open to that and keep yourself open to other people's perspectives, it's such a source of growth, both personally and professionally."

Background

When Kim Scott joined C.J. Abell and Co in 1992, he brought with him five years experience in defence. The small company, originally started by Chris Abell to solve difficult mechanical engineering problems of South Australian clients, was already working with the DSTO. Over the years, this expanded to include major defence projects. The most significant stages of development for the business were the result of winning bigger and bigger defence contracts. During these growth spurts, the business also continued to win smaller (less than $5 million) technology development contracts with defence and DSTO, underpinning the growing skills and capabilities of the business.

In the mid to late 1990s, more effort was put into developing project management and systems engineering processes, and these were applied across the entire business. During this time, Kim progressed through several project and business management roles. In 2000, Tenix acquired the company. Kim was appointed General Manager of the Electronic Systems Division in 2003.

The Tenix Group consists of Tenix Defence, Tenix Alliance, Tenix Solutions, Tenix Aviation, Tenix Datagate, Tenix Projects and several affiliates. This Group has annual revenue of approximately $1.5 billion and 4,300 staff. Tenix Defence has approximately 2,400 staff, $720 million annual revenue and more than $1.3 billion in orders. Its Electronic Systems Division (ESD) has approximately 280 staff, $52 million annual revenue and three Australian locations.

Products and Services

ESD delivers projects, products and services in the electronic systems domain for the Australian Department of Defence and international defence customers. It is a leading provider of integrated solutions in electronic warfare, network enabled warfare, intelligence, surveillance and reconnaissance systems and simulation. The Division also works in the emerging field of national or homeland security, providing intelligent video systems and information security services to national and international customers. Projects range from concept exploration studies for a few hundred thousand dollars, to operational systems such as radars, optical surveillance systems and weapon training systems worth more than $50 Million. The Division also develops and sells advanced technology products for the global marketplace.

Growth Trends

The company has grown from a revenue base of $24 million (2001) to $52 million (2006).

In the early days it grew through winning more and

bigger projects in the domestic defence market. The ability to deliver these projects on schedule and within budget has seen an average bid win rate of 87% (based on number of bids) and 53% (based on dollars of bids) from 2001 to 2006.

The company has maintained strong links with DSTO, with whom it has collaborated in the development of new technologies. These technologies have subsequently been licensed and their products developed for sale in the international market. This has led to two spin-off companies – Tenix LADS (Laser Airborne Depth Sounder, an airborne bathymetric system to measure the depth of water using a laser) and Tenix Datagate, which sells information security products.

One of the early challenges was evolving from a "cottage" business to an engineering organisation with mature systems and processes. That meant less reliance on the heroics of individuals and implementing systems to support staff and innovation. It was challenging to maintain the culture of the people along with their responsiveness to the market and existing customers.

Another issue has been the Commonwealth Government's attitude to supply. When the Government starts on a process of changing or forming strategy, it often interrupts its buying cycle. This is reflected in the ebb and flow of the business. Recently, defence has shown a preference for sourcing equipment from overseas on the basis that they are tapping into a global supply chain. The market where ESD has traditionally worked is starting to flatten out and ESD is looking at alternative markets for future growth.

Performance

Right from the start, the company performed exceptionally well and achieved compound growth rates of around 30-45% annually. This has slowed in recent years because of increasing competition in the domestic defence electronic systems market.

ESD operates over a wide range of project sizes and typically runs 120-140 projects per year. This means it can be less dependent on the larger defence projects which can take 12-18 months to be awarded after tender submission. The division has been able to weather the peaks and troughs of the defence business, particularly those associated with the impending release of a Defence White Paper or Capability Plan which often halts the release of new projects.

ESD has always operated at the premium end of the market, primarily due to overheads associated with defence security and rigorous practices. Its unique selling proposition is the company's ability to solve difficult engineering problems for which the market is yet to offer a solution. This can spawn the development of unique and niche products for global markets.

ESD has grown because of a belief that they could do things at that next level. While there are risk mitigation processes in place, the size of each project means that if anything goes wrong, the potential for impact on the business is significant. A customised set of procedures guides staff and ensures flexibility to suit projects of any size.

Reflecting a commitment to culture, an annual employee survey measures the level of staff engagement and lists areas for improvement. Several projects have been initiated to promote wellbeing including employee assistance and wellness programs, regular communication sessions and free fruit for all staff throughout the day.

Structure

ESD is a wholly owned subsidiary of Tenix Defence Pty Ltd, which is part of the Australian owned Tenix Group. The General Manager reports to the Executive General Manager of Operations and also has routine dialogue with the CEO of Tenix Defence. The General Manager runs ESD through a Board of Management that comprises the senior management team of the division. The Senior Management Team includes: the Manager Electronic Warfare; the Manager Network Enabled Systems; the Manager Intelligence, Surveillance and Reconnaissance; the Manager Support Systems; the HR Manager; the Engineering Manager; the Financial Controller; the Commercial Manager (Contracts) and Business Development. When the division grows substantially, it will be timely to review and restructure the organisation to reduce the number of direct reports to the General Manager.

Brand

ESD is a systems integrator of advanced technology. This is reflected in its brand statement, "Integrating the Future". It also has an internal brand incorporating seven employee value propositions that are about pushing people's boundaries in their professional life. This brand is integrated with ESD's vision to "innovate, solve and deliver quality technology solutions", and reflects its core passion.

The key to ESD's competitive advantage is staff. Typically in the top 3-5% of their graduating class in engineering or science, ESD's people thrive on the challenge to develop leading edge technology. Innovation is encouraged and rewarded.

ESD's mission is to be a major Australian electronic systems provider delivering high-end technology and products to the global defence and adjacent markets. The major issue for the company and its brand is to maintain a focus in the domestic defence market while they apply the skills they have learned there to new areas such as national security and commercial markets.

ESD's challenge is to accelerate the integration of their intellectual property into several products and then market them globally.

Strategic Issues

The most important issues facing ESD are: finding and retaining staff; identifying the next growth market; developing and selling IP based products globally; reducing reliance on the defence industry and moving to a spread of customers; and maintaining successful outcomes with defence while contending with competition from overseas companies which have significant resources and off-the-shelf products.

INSIGHTS INTO

Growing a Company by Developing a Fantastic Culture

ESD is a remarkable business. It was built on values that prioritise caring about what you do. Its success lies in its capacity to harness the passion of staff to solve customer problems.

The Tenix Group values provide strong foundations. The Division's values are: business savvy technologists; a collegiate style environment; service orientation and responsiveness; openness and honesty; team work based on trust and recognition; earned empowerment; and scaleable and efficient processes.

The biggest challenge has been to maintain the culture as the business grew from five or six people who founded the company, to 280 staff. Several ongoing strategies are used. During induction, the General Manager tells staff the company story. He also talks about the values of ESD including employee value propositions. The company has engaged in a major project of developing an employer brand. This includes an annual staff survey and ongoing work with existing staff to facilitate attracting new staff.

Related to this has been the development of the top team and staff throughout the organisation. The top team works on strategy at an annual offsite workshop for several days each year. A strategy is developed with succinct long-term goals and annual objectives that are measured on a bimonthly basis. A traffic light score is given for each of the objectives to determine whether they are on track or not. The top team and other teams also undertake ongoing personal development through external and internal mentoring.

The most important factor has been the development of the General Manager. He has taken a very active approach to personal development, attended courses and worked with coaches. There has also been group and individual mentoring through TEC.

In summary, the secrets of ESD's success are related to the passion and commitment of a leader and his team; a compelling vision; a set of living values; being courageous enough to challenge paradigms; living in the real world of delivering results; dealing with others with authenticity and integrity; and being willing to confront and deal with tough issues in a caring way.

Operating as a CEO

WHAT ARE THE SECRETS OF YOUR SUCCESS AS A CEO?

I think, first and foremost, it's understanding the business. I'd say the other thing is a reasonable balance of hard and soft skills. I've got a strong technical background as well as a reasonable affinity with people and cultural issues – what makes people passionate about their work and how to keep them motivated.

My job is to give them space in which to create and innovate and the freedom to express themselves. That's what they want in their job and that's why they come to work.

What does successful CEO thinking take?

You've got to be able to step outside your business and look around. It's imperative to seek the opinions of others. Learning is a big part of my experience and I've done a lot of work on self-learning. I think you've got to constantly open yourself up to new things and new experiences, realising you'll never stop learning. You also need to take on advice and different perspectives.

What are the biggest challenges and opportunities of being a great CEO?

Challenges: Wanting to do everything myself – I've struggled with delegation; avoiding burnout and acknowledging the need for balance as I get older; and making time to think about the business and not be consumed by operational issues.

Opportunities: There are significant opportunities for personal growth in experiencing something new – for example, an acquisition. Another

opportunity is taking what's been successful in one market into a new market, and experiencing the freshness of that new market. Moving into a new space can revitalise your passion.

What is the one thing, if it could be done, that would have the greatest impact on you as a CEO?

Being given a bigger business opportunity would force me to pull myself out of the detail; and working in a different environment would just take me to that next level.

What has been your biggest disappointment as a CEO?

In the business I'm in, a tender lost is a big disappointment. You put a lot of time and effort into projects and they can run for five or six months. Some bids cost millions, and the reward is high if you win, but when you lose, it's almost like a death. You grieve for a little while and then you need to get over it; almost have a wake and move on.

What key decisions have led to your success?

Implementing a project management methodology and more structured system engineering processes, while taking care not to overdo it and risk stifling the innovation that's helping you grow. Finding the right balance is important because it makes you less reliant on an individual but still allows that individual the space to create, grow and maximise the opportunities available.

How many hours a week do you work?

Up to 80, which is not sustainable in the long-term. But I actually love it.

How do you plan?

Quarterly planning gives me that helicopter view as opposed to chasing the operational issues. I find that weekly planning allows a whole lot of urgent stuff to creep into that week and overrun me. If I step back, I can actually see the critical things that must be achieved in this quarter.

What are the major factors in your role as a CEO that have helped you, hindered you and blocked change?

Helped you: Passionate people who share the vision for the business.

Hindered you: Imposed layers of bureaucracy that don't add value and over which you have no power.

Blocked change: Again, the culprit is bureaucracy.

What part has innovation played in your company?

Innovation is probably the cornerstone of our business. We encourage it through reward and recognition and through a process of funding new ideas.

What is your succession plan?

We have a formal succession process. We look at our people and identify rising stars and good people who need to turn their hand to different roles. Ultimately, it would be my goal to hand over to someone from within the business. If I have to bring someone external in, then I've failed to some extent.

What is your exit strategy?

At 42, I'm relatively young. I'd like to retire mid- to late-50s. I see over a period of time I'll need a new challenge. I'll have to move somewhere else just to broaden my horizons, so that will be my exit.

What is business success to you?

Success is not having to ask people to work back. They want to work back because they love what they're doing. Financial performance is a clear measure of success, but you know you've made it when you have to kick people out at the end of day because they want to be there.

What problems do you, as a CEO, talk about on a day-to-day basis?

People; project and business strategies; how to win the next job; and what the market is saying.

What are the issues that you have to deal with in your leadership role as a CEO?

The interplay between leading a team as well as managing upwards and outwards; and organisational politics.

How has individual and group mentoring helped you?

Having access to many different perspectives has been very helpful, as has getting away. I've gone away for a two-week immersion program where you're living and breathing with other general managers and CEOs who are solving problems, running business relations. Different viewpoints are invaluable for personal development.

What changes have you observed in the workplace culture to remain competitive to employ Generation Y?

We offer employee assistance programs and respond to generation Y's interest in social responsibility through community work. We do a lot of work with primary and secondary schools to encourage students to study maths and science, with the hope they will go on and study engineering.

What impact has the business had on your life?

The negative impact is the time I don't spend with my family and friends. The positive impact is I'm well rewarded. It's allowed me to travel and experience living in America for a couple of years. It's meant my wife hasn't had to go to work – she spends her time bringing up our young children. The positives have outweighed the negatives, but I do need more balance and more time to enjoy with my family.

Do you have to sacrifice your own life and family to be successful in business? Any comments?

Invariably you do, especially in the early stages. As you get over those growth curves, you can then start enjoying the benefits of having put in more up front.

How have you capitalised on your business and developed it in an extraordinary way, geometrically?

We've always believed in ourselves in this business. We're consistent and confident and we've always been a highly motivated, highly intelligent group of people who rise to the next challenge. Sometimes we've been caught out, but I think what we've always done is step up to that next level. I think that's allowed us to do extraordinary things. We have never been constrained by the past.

How has your development as a leader maximised your impact on all of the stakeholders you work with?

I've tried to encourage people to have their say and then once they've all had their say, bring together those views, make a decision and move forward. I then enroll people in that decision.

How has your life developed to make you a better person and how have you maximised this?

A lot of what I've read about or learnt professionally can be applied to my personal life as well. I can take home attitudes about communication, about listening generously without judgment and about commitment. I can make a commitment to my wife and say: "This is my commitment". Then my wife will say: "Okay, if you've committed to that, I'll commit to doing this". It's worked well.

Lessons you have Learned as a CEO

Anxiety leads to action; go where the pain is.

The best leaders work in at least four dimensions – vision, reality, ethics and courage.

Acknowledge accomplishments regularly.

Leaders get the behaviours they tolerate.

People do business with people they like. Becoming powerfully connected and related to people sets up extraordinary outcomes.

Don't look backwards as you go forward. Learn from the past, but don't allow it to determine your future.

Try at every opportunity to listen generously. Listen to people; seek to understand their point of view before you start talking.

Ultimately, people will operate in the space that you give them. Set generous boundaries.

Challenge people and give them choice. To paraphrase a wise old saying: "If you want someone to build a ship, don't teach them how to saw down a tree; teach them passion for the sea".

Your attitude is a conscious decision. Choose it.

Ask yourself: "What are you waiting for?" It's very easy to allow yourself to make excuses for why you haven't acted.

You've got to allow your people to "fail forward". This allows them to learn and exercise personal initiative.

It is important to be "a failure-tolerant leader" – failing is one of the greatest arts in the world. One fails toward success.

The social operating mechanisms of decisive corporate culture feature behaviours marked by four characteristics: openness, candor, informality and closure.

Kim Scott

Final Word

It's often talked about: always open yourself up to new learning. Never believe you will stop learning. You will stop learning the day you die. I think if you keep yourself open to that and keep yourself open to other people's perspectives, it's such a source of growth, both personally and professionally.

Questions for Contemplation

As you reflect on Kim's life ask yourself:

1. How committed are you to what you do? Because commitment really does deliver the results.

2. How have you generated, leveraged and looked for ideas that will produce significant outcomes?

3. Have you allowed yourself to be held back by your past? If so, how are you going to move forward?

4. What is your balance of life? What are you manifesting?

Favorite Book

The Leadership Pipeline: How to Build the Leadership-Powered Company, by Ram Charan, Stephen Drotter and James Noel

Contact Details

Kim Scott - General Manager

Electronic Systems Division

Tenix Defence Pty Ltd

Email: kim.scott@tenix.com

Website: www.tenix.com

Facing the Challenge of Manufacturing in Australia in a Multinational Group

How would you grow a manufacturing company in a competitive environment?

Chris Stathy

Born: 1947

Education: Year 12, Bunbury High School; Diploma in Accounting, Technical Education College, Perth; Philips International Marketing Program, University of Melbourne; MBA, University of South Australia.

Career: Various roles at Philips Industries, 1968-79; Regional Manager (WA), Phillips Industries, 1980-85; General Manager, Sales and Marketing, Amcap Parts, Perth, 1985-88; Sales Director, Federal Mogul, Melbourne, 1988-93; Sales and Marketing Director, Walker Australia, Adelaide, 1993-97; Sales and Marketing Director, Philmac, Adelaide, 1997-2001; Managing Director, Philmac, Adelaide, 2002-present.

Personal: Away from the office Chris enjoys spending time with his family, reading and playing golf.

"Nobody ever advanced in life by holding on to the past. Reflection is good for learning and wisdom, but in business you've got to let go before you leap forward."

Background

Started by Malcolm Phillips in 1929, Philmac is recognised internationally for the design, manufacture, marketing and distribution of high quality, innovative valves and fittings for pipeline systems and irrigation products. In 1986 the company was sold to UK-based Glynwed PLC. Philmac was next purchased in 2001 by the multinational ETEX, which is based in Belgium. ETEX subsequently split into two companies and Aliaxis (the plastics group) became the owner of Philmac.

Chris Stathy joined Philmac as Sales and Marketing Director in 1997 and was promoted to Managing Director in 2002 when the incumbent left to purchase his own business. Chris welcomed the opportunity to become Managing Director; it was something he always wanted to do. Chris reports to a Regional Director (Asia) who is located in New Zealand.

Products and Services

Philmac focuses on the design, manufacture, marketing and distribution of a range of plastic pipe system products, particularly valves, fittings and some irrigation water emission products. It also sources and distributes a range of products from sister companies to enhance its value proposition in the Australian market.

Growth Trends

Philmac operates within a mature market in Australia and holds significant ground in its core markets – up to 70% market share in some cases. In the five years since Chris Stathy became Managing Director, growth has been steady and ongoing. In 2006, Philmac had a turnover of approximately $70 million and 320 staff operating from eight locations (one manufacturing and seven distribution centres). It had grown from a base of $56 million in 2003. Over the next three years, staff numbers will plateau as the manufacturing plant becomes more automated. Return on capital employed is high and rising steadily, as is EBIT.

Philmac is part of the $3 billion Aliaxis group, which consists of a range of companies primarily in Europe and North America. As a group, Aliaxis is seeking acquisitions that will allow it to leverage its products, resources and capabilities in new markets. Its growth strategy therefore is to acquire new businesses within the Australian/New Zealand region that are synergistic with the current operating companies.

The right acquisitions will provide access to the Australia/New Zealand market for group products from overseas. Not only will new acquisitions bring new products to the company but also new intellectual property that can be taken to overseas markets and leveraged in other group companies throughout the world. There is great potential for Philmac to become a $100 million company and dominate its industry sector.

Performance

When Chris Stathy became Philmac's MD in 2002, Australia had experienced the lead up to the worst drought in the country in 100 years. The business was tired. It was suffering from limited investment in people development. The distribution facilities were far too small for the volume of business. Philmac's sales administration activities were fragmented and uncoordinated around Australia. No major new products had been developed or launched since 1995. Innovation had been limited to small, incremental improvements to the existing product range.

Even though automation had been introduced in manufacturing in 1997, it had failed to deliver on cost reduction. In addition, the culture was poor with little or no understanding in the business of total quality management concepts as well as a reluctance to adopt new ways of doing things. Much of the manufacturing machinery was either run down or poorly maintained. Staff engagement was poor. Many good staff had given up and sunk into complacency. The IT systems and networks were like a patchwork quilt. The field sales people were left largely to their own devices.

Export markets were tired. Key markets such as North America, Ireland, and in part, the UK, were being supplied with products that were rapidly becoming outdated. Moreover, the Australian market was facing a downturn in the order of 25% because of water restrictions.

While it was a profitable business, Philmac was facing significant challenges because very little had been done in the past to think about the future. After Chris Stathy became Managing Director in 2002, several key actions were taken. His goal was to build the foundations for a sustainable competitive advantage in the future. Considerable organisational changes were made including: restructuring Manufacturing Management; appointing a new General Manager for Sales and Distribution for Australia to focus on growth and profitability; appointing a new HR Manager and reorganising the human resources function to increase people development and engagement; rearranging the marketing to focus on product market segments with the key role of business development; and appointing an Export Manager with strong technical and target market knowledge.

Philmac also pitched for and won the Hunter distribution business. Regional sales and distribution centres were relocated into larger premises to allow for growth. Customer service was centralised and made fully electronic to maximise efficiency. A new national distribution centre was established which reduced costs and allowed room for growth. Several new products were introduced including a new range of core products for global markets.

Implementing the latest automation techniques has increased flexibility in manufacturing and will enable a 25% reduction of the production work force over the next 18 months. Accompanying this has been a great focus on training and people development in terms of quality, occupational health and safety, product knowledge and management. The company has introduced a management development program which allows managers to undertake studies from Certificate to Diploma level leading to a Masters degree. This will help develop the intellectual capability of the business.

The company regained control of its UK operation in 2005 and is now establishing this as the base for expansion into Europe. The UK business has grown by 35%. The North American distribution business has also been re-established.

In short, Philmac has been transformed. It has become a world class company and is recognised as such by a swag of awards including: a Business SA Export Award, 2003; a Business SA High Achievement Export Award, 2004; An Export Development Award, 2005; and a Marketing Excellence Award, 2006.

Structure

The business is overseen by a Board comprised of the Managing Director, the Chief Financial Officer and the Regional Director in New Zealand. The company is run by a senior management team of eight people who report to the CEO. This team comprises the CFO, the HR Manager, the Manufacturing Manager, the Product Development and Quality Manager, the Marketing Manager, the Export Manager, the Sales and Distribution Manager Australia and the Sales and Distribution Manager UK/Europe.

Brand

Philmac has been in the market for 77 years and has a highly regarded international brand. First and foremost Philmac's brand stands for integrity, honesty and reliability. Also of great importance is product innovation. Philmac's philosophy of finding "a better way" drives every aspect of the company. Thirdly, Philmac is focused on enhancing the capacity of its people.

Brand development must be accompanied by profitable

growth and this has occurred in several ways. The Australian business has grown through the addition of new products and increased volume of existing products. This has been accomplished through the much-improved infrastructure. Increased volume has been achieved without added cost to cover markets in plumbing, building, rural and irrigation.

The Australian business has also implemented strategies to expand into new markets in the mining, industrial and municipal sectors. Another strategy has been to take the new product range into export markets.

Integral to this growth is a manufacturing strategy to reduce the cost of production without compromising the products' integrity. This requires the development of new product that is high in performance but involves lower complexity in manufacturing. Thus there is the need for increased automation in manufacturing as well as process improvement.

Strategic Issues

The most important strategic issues facing Philmac are plastic injection moulding costs, availability of water supply in markets, and infrastructure costs.

INSIGHTS INTO

Successful Manufacturing in Australia in a Multinational Group

The secret of Philmac's success is related to the change process implemented when Chris Stathy became Managing Director. Guided by a clear strategic intent he changed key people and began to develop the culture of the business around its passion for the market and its position of integrity and trustworthiness.

The tag line "The connection you can trust" represents Chris's driving desire for a company customers can trust to deliver a product that will meet their performance expectations; to deliver on time; to respond well to their enquiries; to listen to their concerns; to offer value for money; to be honest in everything; to contribute to the community; to respect the environment and to comply with legal obligations.

It started with getting the leadership group right, engaging them and developing them alongside engaging the workforce. Focus and accountability of staff has been critical. Efficiency has been improved by upgrading the distribution facilities, improving automation in manufacturing and new product development. Operating costs have decreased 12%. Doing more with less and being more efficient has created a capacity for growth through reinvestment. A potential new core product range, at 30% lower cost, has been developed.

Such an outcome was thought to be impossible but it has been achieved. While much progress has been made, there is still work to be done on quality culture, production costs, operating costs and export market development. The culture of Philmac is underpinned by constructive feedback and candor among the management team. Chris has developed a culture that supports people in speaking their minds.

Philmac also has a flexible view about manufacturing. It regards itself as first and foremost a marketing and distribution company. Product can be made and sourced from anywhere so the location of the plant will be determined by the economics and feasibility at the time.

WHAT ARE THE SECRETS OF YOUR SUCCESS AS A CEO?

To live the vision, guide the strategy, monitor progress. Make sure we learn from our mistakes and encourage risk taking. Communicate with all the key stakeholders – customers, owners, community.

We need to make sure that we're always challenged to do things better, and that we celebrate and recognise achievements. Put capable people in positions that allow them to realise their capability and then give them the resources. Get out of their way, but keep communicating with them. That's my management style.

What does successful CEO thinking take?

I think it's listening to a lot of people and their various views, but then making up your own mind rather than waiting for someone else to do it. At the end of the day, you've got to make a decision. At the same time, ask "why not?" rather than "why?" I am a strong believer in being optimistic.

What are the biggest challenges and opportunities of being a great CEO?

Challenges: Time management, suffering fools, deciding what not to do.

Opportunities: Personally, I think I've still got a lot to learn. Every day is a learning experience, particularly about people and managing people. The rest of it I would consider relatively academic.

What is the one thing, if it could be done, that would have the greatest impact on you as a CEO?

If I had more time to think strategically, it would make a big difference to my effectiveness. It's the relationship between things that are priorities and things that are urgent and important. People say,

"Do the important things and forget the urgent things", but it's not quite like that, particularly when you're not in total control. Sometimes I neglect non-urgent strategic thinking.

What has been your biggest disappointment as a CEO?

Times when I've relied on people and perhaps expected too much and they haven't delivered. Fortunately, it hasn't happened very often.

What key decisions have led to your success?

Taking a personal interest in what we're doing in the UK has made a big difference. It's been very successful and we've got an exceptionally good manager there, and between us we work as a great team.

How many hours a week do you work?

Including travel – about 60.

How do you plan?

Generally, weekly on Monday mornings, for maybe

an hour.

What are the major factors in your role as a CEO that have helped you, hindered you and blocked change?

Helped you: My knowledge of finance; my exposure to sales and marketing; my ability to grasp technical issues and understand them.

Hindered you: I'm not a good time manager. I don't think I'm ruthless enough about spending time with people.

Blocked change: When we become over-committed – there's only a certain amount one can do.

What part has innovation played in your company?

Significant in the product development area and considerable in manufacturing and sales. We are trying to become more innovative in all areas of our business.

What is your succession plan?

We are currently working to a plan that ensures I have somebody in a position to step up and take over both short-term and medium-term. There are a couple of options on the go.

What is your exit strategy?

Find a new challenge when the job is done.

What is business success to you?

It's sustainability, profitable growth, contributing positively to the community and also contributing to the people that work in the company, giving them purpose and the ability to realise their potential.

What problems do you, as a CEO, talk about on a day-to-day basis?

Acquisitions, new product introduction, process improvement.

What are the issues that you have to deal with in your leadership role as a CEO?

I need to spend more time with my direct reports to encourage them to develop more. We need to communicate more to make sure that we are completely aligned in terms of vision and the way forward.

How has individual and group mentoring helped you?

It's given me the ability to share a lot of the issues and get some objective input. There are no hidden agendas, which is what you tend to get from people that work for you.

What changes have you observed in the workplace culture to remain competitive to employ Generation Y?

We provide development opportunities for people by making suitable positions available and investing in their education. We're also very big on communication. We run communication sessions every two or three months with all of our people so they know what's going on in the business. We invite people to speak up openly, we have an in-house gym and we're big on health and fitness and wellbeing.

What impact has the business had on your life?

My work has always been very important so the business continues to have an impact on my life. To a large extent, it reflects my values. Sadly, this outlook means I can get dragged along with the way of the world. Sometimes I feel like I want to step off the train and stay on the platform for a while and let it go by, but then you've only got to go and catch up again.

Do you have to sacrifice your own life and family to be successful in business? Any comments?

I think it's about challenging yourself and finding

Chris Stathy

a workable balance. It's hard.

How have you capitalised on your business
and developed it in an extraordinary way,
geometrically?

Basically, by taking a medium-term rather than a
short-term view. We've been prepared to tolerate
the short-term pains for the long-term gains. We've
been in a fortunate position where the company
has been able to afford to do that because we've
improved profitability at the same time.

How has your development as a leader
maximised your impact on all of the
stakeholders you work with?

One thing that has been good for me in this role is
gaining global experience, understanding the way
world markets work. All businesses, regardless of
what anyone says, even the local vegetable grower,
operate in a global market.

How has your life developed to make
you a better person and how have you
maximised this?

In a younger life, I was concerned about building a
career at almost any cost. Now I'm more concerned
about my contribution to the business, to my
family. So my values have changed in that sense,
becoming less focused on me and more focused on
others.

Lessons you have Learned as a CEO

A leopard never changes its spots. People are optimistic that others will change, but they very seldom do in a fundamental sense, particularly when you're talking about performance.

When anyone gives you an opinion about something, ask them to show you. Don't necessarily believe what they say.

You can't rely on everyone. Occasionally, some will let you down. Don't blame them; look at how you manage and communicate with them. Continually check in on people to see how they're going.

Balance, and learn to switch off.

It's about the journey, not the destination.

Family wellbeing is very important.

Spend time with your parents while they're around and try and get to know them as an adult because one day they're not going to be there.

Don't complain about things without being prepared to do something about it.

When the time is right, step out and prove to yourself that you have capabilities.

When moving on, do it decisively. Burn your bridges and go for it.

Continue with your education and put it into practice. It will develop your confidence and your capabilities.

Chris Stathy

Final Word

At the end of the day, you've got to trust people. Don't lose that trust, even though you might get let down sometimes. You can't do it all yourself. Put your effort into leading the people rather than trying to do their job.

Questions for Contemplation

As you reflect on Chris's life ask yourself:

1. What events or influences have challenged your thinking?

2. How relevant are your values to the future?

3. What is your balance of life? What do you need to change?

4. What are you doing to develop personally? How much are you investing in your own development?

5. What attitude do you have towards people? How do you need to change?

Favorite Books

Old Soldiers Never Die: The Life of Douglas MacArthur, by Geoffrey Perret

A Short History of the World, by Geoffrey Blainey

Contact Details

Chris Stathy - Managing Director

Philmac Pty Ltd

Email: chriss@philmac.com.au

Website: www.philmac.com.au

Thinking and Operating Globally

What do you need to do to become a global player?

Glen Simpson

Born: 1944

Education: Diploma in Agriculture (Honours), Queensland Agricultural College, 1963; B. Science in Agriculture (Honours), University of Queensland, 1968; PhD in Agriculture, University of Queensland, 1974.

Career: United Nations Adviser, Spain, and Lecturer in Soil Science, University of New England (Armidale, NSW) 1975-76; Technical Manager, Reed Irrigation, 1974-79; International Project Manager, SAGRIC International 1979-88; Managing Director, SAGRIC International 1989-2005; SAGRIC was acquired by Coffey International Limited in 2000; Executive Director, Coffey International Limited, 2000-present; CEO, Coffey International Development, 2000-present.

Personal: Glen is married with four children. His interests include travel, gardening and fishing.

"I doubt you can be truly successful in business if you've sacrificed your family to do it. To be a success in business is to be **authentic** as a whole person. If you get the work/family balance wrong, you've seriously **impaired** your ability to succeed."

Company Profile

Coffey International Development (Coffey ID) was established when SAGRIC International was purchased by Coffey International in 2000. It is one of three divisions in Coffey. The others are Coffey Consulting and Coffey Project Management. At the time of acquisition, SAGRIC had a $30 million turnover and 30 staff. Since then SAGRIC has become the Coffey International Development Division with four operating regions covering Asia Pacific, the Middle East, Europe and Africa and the Americas, employing in total more than 500 professionals.

The first phase with Coffey ID was a period of consolidation. For the previous 30 years the company was a commercial operation owned by the South Australian State Government. Ownership by a single commercially listed company clarified the purpose and objectives of the company and added access to capital, a performance focus and growth potential.

The first stage of Coffey ID's growth focused on being an Australian business operating regionally. This took two or three years. The second stage could be described as becoming a regional operation headquartered in Australia and this took another two or three years.

The third phase is to become a global operation and this commenced in 2005/2006. Coffey ID now has a turnover in excess of $100 million as part of the Coffey Group, which has a total turnover of over $300 million.

Products and Services

Coffey ID is in the international development business and delivers services in two ways. One is the discipline in which it operates and the other is the nature of service delivery. Disciplines include health, education, environment, agriculture, security and training, post-conflict stabilisation and recovery, private sector development and public sector development. The service delivery process includes program design, program implementation, procurement and logistics. The areas of operation are predominantly in developing economies.

Initially Coffey ID focused on core competency systems to engage subcontractor expertise. As the organisation moves to a global model, it is acquiring regional companies, building more in-house expertise, and developing systems to meet client expectations from core competencies across the disciplines.

Growth Trends

Coffey ID has grown strongly since the acquisition of SAGRIC in 2000 and the establishment of Coffey ID. From 2001 to 2006, organic growth and acquisitions have seen the company triple in size from $30 million to more than $100 million. As the division expands in each of its four operating regions and acquires other businesses, this growth trend will continue as its size broadens capabilities and opens doors to opportunities for larger projects and new clients.

Performance

The sale was a transformational experience for SAGRIC. While it had performed well before this, when it became Coffey ID, a range of possibilities opened up. There was clarity of purpose, access to capital, new capabilities in the group and new relationships internationally.

During the consolidation stage from 2001-2003, there was a lot to explore and exploit using the existing business model. The next stage relied on the leadership seeing Coffey ID as an Australian company operating regionally. As a result Coffey ID was able to start the next phase of growth through regionalisation. It established regional operations and companies and employed local national staff in those countries to leverage opportunities and to build new relationships. Naturally, the next and current stage is to become truly global.

The big issue for Coffey ID through these growth phases was to get critical mass in the main regions of operation through acquisition and organic growth. This process will continue as Coffey ID establishes itself in more countries and increases its global footprint, critical mass and influence.

Structure

Coffey International is a public company with a Board of five directors. There are three non-executive directors, one of whom is Chair, and two executive directors. Both the Managing Director of the Coffey Group and the CEO of Coffey International Development are on the Board. It is a small but highly effective Board that is not constrained by Directors representing any individual sector of interest. The Board is very particular about corporate governance and operating strictly in accordance with the corporations' law.

The Company has three divisions – Coffey International Development, Coffey Consulting and Coffey Project Management. Under the Board, reporting to the Managing Director is an executive group of eleven including the COOs of the main operating companies, the Corporate Development Officer, plus the Heads of the Support Services of Finance, HR and IT.

With the acquisition of SAGRIC in 2000, Coffey had two major activities – consulting engineering and international development. Through strategic growth and acquisitions, Glen Simpson has led the growth of SAGRIC into Coffey International Development; and Roger Olds has led the overall growth of Coffey and the growth of consulting engineering into Coffey Geotechnics, Environments, Mining and Coffey Project Management.

Coffey International Development is a division of Coffey with four regional operations each run by a Chief Operating Officer reporting to the CEO. These are Coffey ID Asia Pacific; Coffey ID Middle East; Coffey ID Europe and Africa and Coffey ID Americas. The main regional operations each have their own management structure including Managers of Business Development; Corporate Services; Finance and Administration; and Operations.

Brand

The development of the Coffey brand presented the Board with real strategic opportunities.

Coming from a business model of a domestic consulting engineering company, there was a limit to the market interest in a listed company constrained by the cyclical nature of this model. On the other hand, it was not immediately apparent how this business model tied in with a company built on a project management business model in the area of international development.

Following a thorough strategic analysis of possibilities, the answer came when Coffey saw themselves as being in the business of "improving the lives of world communities". They contributed to this outcome by being able to enhance both the physical and social infrastructure of those communities, irrespective of geography.

This breakthrough linked Coffey's operations and provided a clear strategic path for expansion and acquisition to infill areas where Coffey needed more capability or geographic presence.

Their core strengths lay in being the best in class in their chosen fields and exceeding client expectations in the delivery of all services – hence Coffey's motto: "Specialist Knowledge, Extraordinary Outcomes".

Strategic Issues

Strategic issues for Coffey ID include accessing expertise in this industry to satisfy the demand; and providing the physical security, welfare, health and protection of Coffey ID personnel. This is a particular challenge when one considers the more than 50 countries where Coffey ID operates.

Coffey ID, as part of the Coffey group, has developed into a truly international company with a global outreach.

Sadly, natural disasters, instability and conflict create a great demand for services. In the initial humanitarian phase, governments provide emergency relief such as shelter and food. The second phase of recovery, the post-trauma or post-conflict reconstruction phase, focuses on re-establishing the fundamentals for functioning communities. The third phase is the re-establishment or introduction of public sector services and the role of the private sector in development. Most of Coffey ID's services are relevant to the post humanitarian stages.

INSIGHTS INTO

Thinking and Operating Globally

How does an Australian regional organisation become a global operation? The answer lies in how you see what you do, the way you think and talk about what you are, and the way you operate. From the CEO's perspective, as chief strategist you have to see the future, stand in it and make it become a reality. This requires letting go of things in the present to move to a bigger, better future. This is what happened to Glen Simpson in a series of transitions to take Coffey ID to its current position as a global operation.

The other aspect of this was to identify and acquire suitable companies to enable Coffey ID to have a global footprint, acquire extensive in-house expertise, develop the core competencies of regional leaders and invest in the development of systems. As a result this has enabled Coffey ID to think and act globally. Glen Simpson's ongoing role as a leader of change has been critical to enable this to happen and to empower a range of leaders to carry this out and leverage what they have.

WHAT ARE THE SECRETS OF YOUR SUCCESS AS A CEO?

Listening; having a genuine caring interest in individuals; and a natural inclination to explore possibilities. I get excited about possibilities; I get frustrated with operational detail.

What does successful CEO thinking take?

A passion for your industry and the opportunities within it; a willingness to listen with an open mind to ideas about what's possible; and having the courage to create a compelling vision, enroll others in it and then go the distance.

What are the biggest challenges and opportunities of being a great CEO?

Challenges: Owning the far-reaching consequences of your decisions; and keeping up the energy, commitment and enthusiasm.

Opportunities: Every day is exciting in terms of helping people reach their potential and exploring the possibilities of your chosen field.

What has been your biggest disappointment as a CEO?

I'm impatient. I would have liked to have been where I am now 18 months ago, but a lot of people might consider where we're at now is quite an achievement given where it was about four years ago. It's all relative.

How do you handle rejection and failure?

I don't have a difficulty with that because I'm clear about what I stand for and where we're heading. I take a failure as a temporary setback or a diversion, not as an invalidation of the purpose or destination of the journey. I've learned from Leader of the Future (LTF) and The Executive Connection (TEC) that everything that appears like a setback has happened for a purpose. You've got to learn what the purpose was because there is a lesson there. Taking the time to learn that lesson will reinforce your conviction and empower you to achieve your goal. In essence, know what you stand for, create a compelling vision and never give up.

What key decisions have led to your success?

If it is to be, it is up to me. If you want something to happen, you've got to make it happen. If there were any major milestones in my journey, personally and professionally, they were to see myself in a new context and not be constrained by where I had come from. I am now in a position where I am able to leverage five times the level of business of my previous roles and had I not been prepared to let go and move on, I would have been stuck with a multiple of one.

How many hours a week do you work?

More than 60 hours per week, but it is hard to measure because when you travel the work days get very full and include weekends.

How do you plan?

I work backwards from the future. Once you know what the future looks like because you're standing in it, it is then easy to see how you got there.

What are the major factors in your role as a CEO that have helped you, hindered you and blocked change?

Helped you: Getting to know myself and what I stood for.

Hindered you: The time it's taken to fully understand the principles of standing in the future and applying them in my life and work.

Blocked change: The biggest constraint to my growth as a CEO was not knowing enough about myself and what I stood for. That was one of the things that came out of my experience with LTF – first know yourself.

What part has innovation played in your company?

Seeing the needs of clients before they have, and, obviously, IT plays a major role in innovation in a global organisation.

How and when have you transitioned your role?

From SAGRIC International MD to CEO of Coffey International Development, and, more importantly, from operational to strategic leadership.

What is your succession plan?

Within the new global structure we have very competent regional managers, any one of whom can fulfil my role in time.

What is your exit strategy?

With the globalisation of our international development business over the next 3 to 5 years, I would be looking to wind back a bit and become more of a mentor. I want to stay engaged with the corporate world, but not 60 hours a week.

What is business success to you?

Seeing the growth of young people to a level where they can run businesses and engage with environmental issues better than our generation did. It's all to do with personal growth.

What problems do you, as a CEO, talk about on a day-to-day basis?

Helping operational managers stay aligned with visionary priorities in their decision making; talking to people as individuals and understanding their needs. A CEO has to keep a finger on the financial performance pulse for any early signs of issues.

What are the issues that you have to deal with in your leadership role as a CEO?

I focus on inspirational leadership and resist giving operational advice, otherwise you can give misleading guidance if you don't have all the facts and you run the risk of developing a dependency culture.

How do you allow the space and time for creative thinking for yourself and your staff?

Exploring possibilities is a 24/7 hobby. Creativity is something you live – it's you. It's not a matter of blocking out an hour in the diary. It's a lifestyle. Every time I'm driving, or sitting by the pool, I am engaged in reflection and creative thinking.

How has individual and group mentoring helped you?

It helps you keep a perspective on your priority and to be accountable for your plans. You learn a

Glen Simpson

lot from others but if you stop learning and stop growing personally, your creativity is dying. You never want to think that you know all there is to be known in your field. The more you learn, the more you need to learn, so always look for the opportunity to engage with a new challenge and push out your comfort zones. I have found that TEC and the coaching that comes with it continually provide me with new challenges.

What changes have you observed in the workplace culture to remain competitive to employ Generation Y?

I think the next generations of managers have characteristics that are different from one another as individuals, and they are so different from our generation that it's really exciting for the future. They see challenges and possibilities from a totally different perspective. Accordingly, I believe that it is critical to engage and consult with people at all levels and age groups in planning processes.

What impact has the business had on your life?

Because the business we're involved in is focused on making a difference in the world, I see everything more in a global context than in a local context. We are privileged to be in this industry and the importance of helping to improve the lives of world communities has never been more evident than it is today.

Do you have to sacrifice your own life and family to be successful in business? Any comments?

No, absolutely not. I doubt you can be truly successful in business if you've sacrificed your family to do it. To be a success in business is to be authentic as a whole person. If you get the work/family balance wrong, you've seriously impaired your ability to succeed.

How have you capitalised on your business and developed it in an extraordinary way, geometrically?

By stepping back from the operational dimension, analysing and understanding where we're having the greatest impact on communities and then looking at ways to leverage that. This means putting my energies into replicating globally what we're doing very effectively at a national and regional level.

How has your development as a leader maximised your impact on all of the stakeholders you work with?

By trying to set an inspirational example of what is possible for anybody. Put in the hard yards to understand yourself and what you stand for so that you can remove the blockages and impediments that come with self-interest and ego.

How has your life developed to make you a better person and how have you maximised this?

By understanding the principle that having and showing a genuine interest in others takes care of any self-interest issues you might have had. So, if you come from the point of view of caring and interest in others, then your needs are fulfilled.

Lessons you have Learned as a CEO

You can only achieve significant outcomes through others.

Clarity of vision about where you're heading as an individual and organisation is critical.

Consider all possibilities that people propose as being valid.

Don't prejudge others.

Enthusiasm is the greatest motivator as a leader.

Be genuinely interested in and care for people and employees.

Learn to see the world through others' eyes.

First seek to understand, then to be understood.

Client and other stakeholder relationships are fundamental to growth and sustainability.

You are not your job.

Do whatever it takes to deliver and never give up on a worthwhile goal.

Glen Simpson

Final Word

The two things I keep coming back to are caring and having a genuine interest in others, and having a passion for creating a vision around possibilities. The world needs people who invest experience and energy into creating a compelling vision and then care enough about people to get alignment with that vision.

Questions for Contemplation

Glen challenges you to look inside yourself to see what you really care enough about to want to make a difference with your life. To do this, be prepared to make the investment in first understanding yourself.

1. How much do you want to make a difference with your life? Have you discovered the real purpose for your life?

2. How prepared are you to make the necessary investment in understanding yourself and what you stand for before you can begin trying to make a difference for others?

3. What is your compelling vision for your future, for your business and what are the possibilities for your business?

4. How much are you willing to sacrifice to achieve this and how will you make choices to give your life balance?

Favorite Book

Good to Great by Jim Collins

Contact Details

Glen Simpson - Executive Director

Coffey International Limited

Email: Glen_Simpson@coffey.com.au

Website: www.coffey.com.au

Conclusion

As we conclude this book, one might ask, "What were the major themes?" Here is a summary:

Practise leadership – vision plus action plus passion. When a leader imagines and mentally stands in the future, he or she then creates that vision. Projection is a powerful tool.

Clarify and implement your strategy. One of the most important roles of a CEO is to be the Chief Strategist.

Create an evolving management structure to enable the business to grow. Having the right hand-picked team who develop along with the business is critical for success.

It is important to create a robust climate of teamwork, great communication and strong feedback so that staff can say what they mean and mean what they say. There is no room for "Yes people" in growing companies committed to excellence, continuous improvement and outstanding achievement. Only integrity, authenticity and openness are relevant.

It is essential to have the correct internal capability in a company. When a company grows it quite often outstrips the capacity of its staff, information technology, marketing, operations, systems and finance. It is critical to continue to reinvent and be ahead of the game if your company is going to be able to survive the growth spurts.

Succession planning for all companies is absolutely critical and an important theme particularly for family companies. CEOs must decide what they want to do, when they will transition and what altered or reduced role they will want to take in the future, if they continue in the company.

Life balance and impact on the family was a recurring theme in the book. The CEO role is one of the most challenging roles in business. It has the capacity to demand your total life if you let it. It is critical that CEOs face this head-on and allocate time each year for holidays, time each month for recreation and time each week for their family. You must be able to enjoy the moment and to be with yourself – remember the concept of a human doing versus a human being: to be and not to do. How sad to have spent your time on this earth as a person who mistook his job for his life.

Another major theme was hard work versus smart work. Even if you work smart, have a great team and can delegate well, you are nevertheless required to reconcile the demands of the role, the competing needs of stakeholders (shareholders, managers, staff, suppliers, customers, banks and government) and your own needs as well as that of your family. It is a lot of hard work, which is unavoidable in such a demanding role.

Mentoring is a powerful, recurring theme throughout the book. Why is mentoring so important? Mentors help CEOs change effectively and the intensity of change will increase in the future. Excellent mentors are positive change agents and inspire CEOs to develop new hope, purpose and to take major actions. The value of having a sounding board is inestimable for CEOs because it *is* lonely at the top. The incredible experience of belonging to a quality peer group to experience validation, benchmarking, care, support and challenge has enormous benefits to anyone willing to be open to give and receive.

And, finally, we must not forget the incredible qualities of persistence and determination as being the basic ingredients for becoming and remaining a successful CEO. As Napoleon once said, "Victory belongs to the most persevering!" How right he was… and is!

Suggested Reading

Buckingham, Marcus and Coffman, Curt – *First, Break All The Rules: What the World's Greatest Managers Do Differently*

Buckingham, Marcus and Clifton, Donald O. – *Now, Discover Your Strengths*

Buckingham, Marcus – *The One Thing You Need To Know… About Great Managing, Great Leading, and Sustained Individual Success*

Buford, Bob – *Half Time: Changing Your Game Plan from Success to Significance*

Caldini, Robert B. – *Influence – The Psychology of Persuasion*

Collins, Jim and Porras, Jerry I. – *Built to Last – Successful Habits of Visionary Companies*

Collins, Jim. – *Good to Great: Why Some Companies Make the Leap… and Others Don't*

Frankel, Victor E. – *Man's Search For Meaning*

Gerber, Michael E. – *The E-Myth Revisited: Why Most Small Businesses Don't Work and What to Do About*

Hanson, Mark Victor and Allen, Robert G. – *The One Minute Millionaire*

Hill, Napoleon – *Think and Grow Rich*

Hudson, Frederic M. – *The Handbook of Coaching: A Comprehensive Resource Guide for Managers, Executives, Consultants, and Human Resource Professionals*

Kim, W. Chan and Mauborgne, Renée – *Blue Ocean Strategy*

Lencioni, Patrick M. – *The Five Dysfunctions of a Team: A Leadership Fable*

Levoy, Gregg – *Callings: Finding and Following an Authentic Life*

Kiyosaki, Robert T. – *Rich Dad, Poor Dad*

Olivier, Richard – *Inspirational Leadership: Henry V and the Muse of Fire – Timeless Insights from Shakespeare's Greatest Leader*

Palmer, Parker J. – *Let Your Life Speak: Listening for the Voice of Vocation*

Pfeffer, Jeffrey and Sutton, Robert I. – *The Knowing-Doing Gap: How Smart Companies Turn Knowledge into Action*

Robinson, Bryan E. – *Chained to the Desk: A Guide for Workaholics, Their Partners and Children, and the Clinicians Who Treat Them*

Treacy, Michael and Wiersema, Fred – *The Discipline of Market Leaders: Choose Your Customers, Narrow Your Focus, Dominate Your Market*

Vaill, Peter B. – *Learning as a Way of Being: Strategies for Survival in a World of Permanent White Water*

Warren, Rick – *The Purpose Driven Life*

Reader Gifts

As a reader of *Secrets of Successful CEOs*, you are invited to visit www.secretsofceos.com and enjoy some fabulous bonuses. Simply visit the site and follow the prompts to receive the following downloads for free …

Gift 1

Leverage your life, leadership, business and community 100x
By Adrian Geering

Gift 2

Leadership Development Strategies
By Adrian Geering

Gift 3

Survival Strategies – The steps to take to maintain a healthy business
By Adrian Geering

www.secretsofceos.com

Also by Adrian Geering

CEOs on CD with Adrian Geering

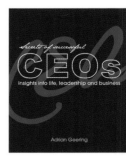

Introducing the faces behind the Secrets of Successful CEOs – Insights into Life, Leadership and Business in audio, up close and personal.

Here, Dr Geering asks tough, pointed and intriguing questions of his subjects in 20 candid interviews, and is himself interviewed about his journey to international mentor and coach, the road of all CEOs and the true secrets to flourishing at the top.

Interviews available from www.secretsofceos.com

Lessons on Leadership and Business

Lessons on Leadership and Business is a collection of poignant leadership lessons and insights on business that will inspire, challenge and evoke. Compiled by Adrian Geering, and taken from his insights gained in his Secrets of Successful CEOs, this book has the hidden information of business leaders in a compact format. Don't travel the journey of life and business alone. Take advice from great Australian CEOs from all walks of life and business.

**This book is also available from
www.secretsofceos.com**